111 Homemade Rice Pudding Recipes

(111 Homemade Rice Pudding Recipes - Volume 1)

Jane Wilson

Content

111 Awesome Rice Pudding Recipes

***

1. A Stirring Rice Pudding Recipe

Serving: 8 | Prep: | Cook: 60mins | Ready in:

Ingredients

- Basic recipe ingredients:
- 3/4 cup short grain rice (Egyptian rice)
- 1 cup water to cook rice
- 8 cups milk at room temperature
- 1 cup sugar
- 1/2 cup rose water
- mastic
- 1/2 cup ground pistachios.
- Optional: raisins, toasted chopped nuts , shredded coconut , vanilla ice cream.

Direction

- Wash rice well, let it soak in warm water for 1 hour.
- Place rice in a large pot, add one cup water, and let it boil
- After 10 minutes add milk and keep stirring, this is the hectic part of this recipe, it takes 45 minutes.
- Stir in sugar so it won't burn at the bottom of the pot leave it for 5 more minutes keep stirring.
- Crush mastic with 1 Tbsp. of sugar, add it to the pot,
- Stir rose water in.
- Remove from heat.
- Spoon in individual bowls, sprinkle ground pistachios.
- Serve warm or cold.

- Note: The authentic recipe calls for both rose water and mastic, substituting rose water with vanilla is an option. You may stir in raisins and shredded coconut.
- Presentation: Served in individual bowls, warm with a scoop of vanilla ice cream, toasted nuts. I liked mine cold with a sprinkle of cinnamon.

2. Almond And Mascarpone Rice Pudding With Vanilla Recipe

Serving: 8 | Prep: | Cook: 15mins | Ready in:

Ingredients

- 1 cup sliced or slivered almonds, divided
- 1 L carton almond beverage, about 4 cups
- 2½ cups whipping cream
- 1 cup arborio or other Italian short-grain rice
- 3/4 cup granulated sugar, divided
- ¼ tsp salt
- ¼ to ½ vanilla bean or 1½ tsp pure vanilla extract
- 3 eggs
- ½ cup mascarpone cheese

Direction

- Preheat oven to 350°F
- Spread out almonds on a dry tray; bake 5 to 8 minutes or until golden. Cool on a rack. Finely chop half the almonds; set all separately aside.
- Combine almond beverage, whipping cream, rice, 1/2 cup sugar and salt in a large saucepan. Split vanilla bean lengthwise; scrape out seeds. Add pod and seeds to rice mixture. (If using extract, do not add.)
- Cook over medium-high heat, stirring constantly for 8 to 10 minutes, or just until mixture begins to simmer.
- Reduce heat as needed to between medium and medium-low.

- Gently bubble, partially covered and stirring frequently, especially near the end of cooking time, for 35 minutes or until rice is tender and mixture is very creamy.
- Take out and discard vanilla pod.
- Remove pan from heat.
- Beat eggs with remaining ¼ cup sugar with a whisk in a small bowl until just combined.
- Stirring constantly, whisk in several spoonfuls of hot rice mixture; then whisk egg mixture back into remaining rice mixture in pan.
- Return to medium-low heat, stirring constantly for 2 to 3 minutes to cook eggs and thicken pudding.
- Stir in chopped almond and spoonfuls of mascarpone cheese — and vanilla extract, if using.
- Serve warm or at room temperature. (Or lay a piece of plastic directly on pudding surface; refrigerate for up to 2 to 3 days. If cold pudding thickens too much for your taste, thin with milk.)
- Serve sprinkled with remaining toasted almonds and sliced kumquats or other colourful fruit.

3. Almond Milk Rice Pudding Recipe

Serving: 8 | Prep: | Cook: 60mins | Ready in:

Ingredients

- 1/2 cup raw rice
- 4 cups organic almond milk- it's a non dairy almond beverage
- 4 to 6 Tbs pure maple syrup or as desired
- 1/4 c fine crushed natural unsalted almonds
- 1 tsp cinnamon or to taste
- dash salt
- Garnish: optional: non dairy whipped topping

Direction

- In heavy duty pot, place rice, almond milk, cinnamon, salt, maple syrup and bring to a boil.
- Then reduce heat and cook and stir very frequently at a low bubble until rice has absorbed liquid and has become soft and tender.
- Adjust sweetness if desired to taste
- Remove from burner, cover and cool to room temp
- Then chill well
- Note: when cooling this pudding will not get any thicker than the finished product, there is no fat or dairy
- May serve warm or chilled

4. Apple Rice Pudding Recipe

Serving: 8 | Prep: | Cook: 45mins | Ready in:

Ingredients

- 2 eggs
- 1/2 cup sugar
- 1/4 teaspoon salt
- 1/2 cup sour cream
- 1-1/4 cups evaporated milk
- 2-1/2 cups cooked rice
- 1 granny smith apple peeled, cored and chopped
- 1 cup shredded medium sharp cheddar cheese
- 1/2 cup raisins
- 1/4 cup firmly packed brown sugar
- 1 tablespoon all purpose flour
- 1 teaspoon cinnamon
- 1 tablespoon melted margarine

Direction

- Combine first five ingredients in a bowl then stir in rice, apples, cheese and raisins.
- Spoon into a lightly greased square baking dish.
- Combine brown sugar, flour, cinnamon and margarine then sprinkle over rice mixture.

- Bake uncovered at 350 for 45 minutes.

5. Apple And Rice Pudding Recipe

Serving: 6 | Prep: | Cook: 50mins | Ready in:

Ingredients

- 2 cups water
- 1 cup uncooked long grain brown rice
- 2 cups milk
- 1 cup heavy cream
- 2 large eggs
- 1/4 cup sugar
- 1/4 teaspoon salt
- 2 large apples peeled cored and coarsely chopped
- 1/2 cup dark raisins
- 1/2 cup dried apricots quartered
- 2 tablespoons vanilla extract

Direction

- In a heavy saucepan heat water to boiling then stir in rice.
- Cover and cook over low heat for 20 minutes.
- Add milk to rice in saucepan and cook 20 minutes stirring occasionally to prevent sticking.
- In small bowl beat cream and eggs with a wire whisk then stir in sugar and salt.
- Whisk into rice mixture along with apples, raisins, apricots and vanilla.
- Cook stirring occasionally until mixture thickens but do not boil.
- Spoon rice mixture into a greased shallow baking dish and bake 30 minutes.
- Serve warm or cold.

6. Arborio Rice Pudding With Rum Raisin Mascarpone Recipe

Serving: 0 | Prep: | Cook: 20mins | Ready in:

Ingredients

- Rum-raisin mascarpone
- 1 cup raisins, packed tightly
- 1 cup sugar
- 1/2 cup dark rum
- 1 lemon, juice only
- 2 cups mascarpone cheese
- 2 cups heavy whipping cream
- Pudding
- 3 cups whole milk
- 2 tablespoons unsalted butter
- 1 cup packed light brown sugar
- 1/2 teaspoon ground cinnamon
- 1 vanilla bean, split and scraped
- 1 cup arborio rice
- Pinch kosher salt
- 1 cup creme fraiche
- lemon zest

Direction

- 1. To prepare Rum-Raisin Mascarpone, soak raisins in a mixture of the granulated sugar, rum, and lemon juice. Muddle (squash) raisins with a wooden spoon to help them soak and rehydrate a little. Set aside while you prepare the rice pudding.
- 2. Put milk, butter, brown sugar, cinnamon, vanilla bean contents, rice, and salt into a large saucepan. Bring to a simmer over medium heat; stirring constantly. Simmer Arborio rice for 20 to 22 minutes, until tender, yet firm (al dente). (The rice mixture should have slightly more liquid than regular risotto.) Remove from heat; stir in crème fraiche.
- 3. Strain the liquid from the raisins; reserve liquid. Combine mascarpone and cream and whisk until light and creamy in a large bowl. Swirl in the strained raisins and drizzle a little of the soaking liquid over top. Garnish rice pudding with lemon zest. Top rice pudding

with a generous spoonful of Rum-Raisin Mascarpone. Serve pudding with additional Rum-Raisin Mascarpone on the side.

7. Armenian Honey Rice Pudding Recipe

Serving: 6 | Prep: | Cook: 60mins | Ready in:

Ingredients

- 1/2 cup rice
- 1 cup sugar
- 1/3 cup honey
- 3 !/2 cups water
- 1/4 tsp ground ginger
- cinnamon
- cloves
- blanched almonds
- walnuts

Direction

- Wash rice and drain.
- Place in pot with water and boil gently 1/2 hour.
- Add 1/3 cup of the sugar and stir.
- Let boil gently another 10 minutes.
- Repeat twice again with the remaining third cups of sugar
- Complete cooking should total about one hour.
- Remove from heat and add ginger and stir.
- Pour into 6 pudding dishes.
- Sprinkle each with cinnamon, ginger and cloves. Decorate with nuts
- Serve hot or cold

8. Arroz Doce Rice Pudding Recipe

Serving: 6 | Prep: | Cook: 25mins | Ready in:

Ingredients

- 1 cup starchy rice (like risotto rice)
- 2 cups water
- grated zest of 1 lemon
- 1 litre full fat milk (or 0.8 of a litre of milk + 0.2 litre carton thick cream)
- 6 egg yolks
- 10 tbsp sugar
- 1 cinnamon stick
- ground cinnamon

Direction

- Cook the rice with the water and cinnamon stick for about 10 minutes, or until the water has been absorbed.
- Remove the cinnamon stick.
- Whisk the egg yolks with the milk (or milk and cream), the sugar and lemon zest.
- Add to the rice and let it cook for about 10 minutes more, in low heat.
- It should be creamy but runny.
- Pour into a large serving dish, or individual ones.
- Sprinkle/decorate with ground cinnamon.
- Serve cold.

9. Baked Rice Pudding Recipe

Serving: 11 | Prep: | Cook: | Ready in:

Ingredients

- 1 cup white rice, uncooked
- 3 eggs, beaten
- 2 cups milk
- 1/3 cup raisins
- 1/2 cup sugar (white)
- 2 cups of water
- 1 tsp vanilla extract
- 1/2 tsp of salt
- 1 pinch nutmeg, ground

Direction

- Put rice, uncooked, into a 3 qt. saucepan, and add water. Once at a boil, reduce the heat, and simmer for 25-30 minutes. Now, preheat the oven to 325 degrees F. Combine milk, sugar, beaten eggs, vanilla extract, and salt in a large sized bowl and mix it well. Next, stir in the raisins and rice. Pour the mixture into a 10x6x2 inch baking dish and bake, uncovered, for 30 minutes. Now, stir the pudding while adding a sprinkle of nutmeg. Finally, bake an additional 30 minutes (or until a knife can be inserted halfway between the edge and the center, and comes out clean.)

10. Barbs Rice Pudding Recipe

Serving: 12 | Prep: | Cook: 120mins | Ready in:

Ingredients

- This makes a large amount. Half the recipe for less.
- 1 pound "Carolina" rice
- 1 stick butter, sweet
- 1 can evaporated milk
- 1 quart milk
- 1 cup sugar or add more or less to taste
- 1 large package of jello instant pudding
- vanilla to taste
- raisins (optional, I soak mine to plump them up then drain them)

Direction

- Boil rice in directed amount of water until almost tender.
- Can leave some water in the pot.
- Turn to simmer.
- Then add butter, can milk, milk, sugar and simmer 2 hours.
- Remove from heat.
- Stir in dry pudding mix add vanilla.
- Raisin should get add in the last 15 minutes of cooking if you are adding them.
- Sprinkle with cinnamon.

11. Best Rice Pudding Recipe

Serving: 6 | Prep: | Cook: 35mins | Ready in:

Ingredients

- 1 cup uncooked rice
- 1 quart milk (I use 1%)
- 1 egg
- 1/2 cup sugar
- 1 tsp vanilla
- raisins & cinnamon (optional)

Direction

- Heat the milk in a large heavy saucepan and then add the rice. Cook over low heat till the rice is soft remembering to stir once in a while. Taste for texture to make sure that it is nice and soft. Remove from the heat.
- Beat the egg with the sugar and vanilla then add some of the rice mixture to temper the eggs and then add them to the rest of the rice milk mixture. Add the raisins if using.
- Pour the mixture into a serving dish and sprinkle with the cinnamon. Cover the surface with plastic wrap making sure to lay it right on top of the rice. You can serve this at whatever temperature you like-slightly warm; room temp or cold from the fridge.
- If you use raisins then put about 1/2 cup into a bowl and pour some boiling water over them and let them sit for a few minutes then drain and squeeze dry.

12. Brown Rice Peanut Butter Pudding Recipe

Serving: 6 | Prep: | Cook: 50mins | Ready in:

Ingredients

- 3 large eggs
- 2 cups brown rice cooked
- 1/2 cup creamy peanut butter
- 1/3 cup honey
- 1 tablespoon cinnamon
- 2 cups milk
- 1/2 cup dates chopped
- 1/2 cup raisins

Direction

- Combine eggs, cooked rice, peanut butter, honey and cinnamon.
- Stir in milk, raisins and dates then turn into baking dish and place dish in larger dish.
- Add 1" water to larger pan then bake 25 minutes at 350.
- Stir mixture then bake another 25 minutes.
- Top with whipped cream and peanuts if desired.

13. Brown Rice Pudding Recipe

Serving: 6 | Prep: | Cook: 300mins | Ready in:

Ingredients

- brown rice Pudding
- 1/2 cup brown aromatic rice, such as brown jasmine or brown
- basmati
- 1/3 cup dried cranberries
- 1/4 cup sugar
- 1 can light coconut milk, such as Taste of Thai
- 1-1/3 cups nonfat milk
- 1/2 cup liquid egg substitute, such as Egg Beaters
- 1 tsp. almond extract
- 2 bananas, sliced
- optional: brown sugar

Direction

- Spray your slow cooker stoneware with non-stick cooking spray.

- Stir together brown rice, cranberries and sugar in Crockpot stoneware. In a separate bowl, whisk coconut milk, non-fat milk, egg substitute and almond extract together. Pour over rice mixture. Cook on high for four to five hours.
- Serve with sliced bananas and brown sugar on top, if desired.
- Serves 6.

14. Budino Di Riso Rice Pudding Recipe

Serving: 6 | Prep: | Cook: 50mins | Ready in:

Ingredients

- ½ cup arborio rice
- 8 cups whole milk
- ½ cup sugar
- 1 vanilla bean, split lengthwise (or use 1 tsp real vanilla extract)
- 1/4 teaspoon ground cinnamon
- 1/4 teaspoon salt
- 2 large egg yolks
- ½ cup heavy cream
- 2 teaspoons real vanilla extract
- freshly grated nutmeg (optional)
- caramel sauce and/or whipped cream, for serving (optional)

Direction

- Stir together rice, milk, sugar, vanilla bean, cinnamon and salt in a large saucepan over medium-high heat. Bring to a boil, stirring constantly.
- Reduce heat to medium-low and simmer for 30 minutes, stirring every 5 minutes as the mixture starts to thicken.
- Continue to cook until the rice is tender but not too mushy, 15 minutes longer. The milk will be thick and the rice tender, but the mixture should be a little soupy.

- In a bowl, whisk together 2 egg yolks and cream and stir into cooked rice.
- Continue to cook over medium-low heat for 2 to 3 minutes, until eggs are cooked through and pudding is creamy and glossy but still fairly soupy.
- Remove from heat and stir in remaining vanilla extract. Grate a little nutmeg in, if you like.
- Remove the vanilla bean, if you've used one.
- Pour the pudding into a bowl and press plastic wrap over the surface to prevent a skin from forming. Refrigerate until cold, 2 to 3 hours.
- Serve pudding as is, or layer in a parfait glass with caramel sauce and top with whipped cream.
- Each serving: about 512 calories; 16 grams protein; 57 grams carbohydrate; 24 grams fat (14 grams saturated); 1 gram fiber; 171 milligrams cholesterol; 320 milligrams sodium.

15. Buttered Rum Raisin Rice Pudding Recipe

Serving: 6 | Prep: | Cook: 20mins | Ready in:

Ingredients

- 2 1/2 cups long grain rice
- 6 cups whole milk
- 2 cups half-and-half
- 1/2 cup dark rum
- 1/2 cup raisins
- 4 tbs butter
- 1 tsp vanilla
- 1/4 tsp salt
- 1 tsp cinnamon
- 4 egg yolks
- 2 1/2 cups sugar

Direction

- In saucepot bring rum, butter and raisins to simmer. Watch pot and do not leave stove or get distracted. If rum ignites, remove from

heat and allow to burn out. Set aside and allow raisins to steep.
- Using a heavy bottom pot combine rice, milk, 1 cup half-and-half, vanilla, salt and cinnamon. Heat to simmer, but do not boil
- Cover and cook until rice is tender, stirring occasionally
- In mixing bowl whisk egg yolks, sugar and remaining cup of half-and-half. Slowly add rice mixture a little at a time whisking constantly so eggs won't scramble.
- Put mixture back in pot and heat slowly until pudding begins to thicken.
- Fold in rum-raisins.
- Be careful at this point and do not boil or stir any more than needed to prevent custard from breaking and becoming dense.
- Serve hot or refrigerate for a cold pudding. Cover with plastic wrap if you refrigerate.

16. CHOCOLATE RICE PUDDING Recipe

Serving: 4 | Prep: | Cook: 10mins | Ready in:

Ingredients

- 4 cups cold milk
- 1 package (3.9 ounces) instant chocolate pudding mix
- 1/4 cup chopped walnuts
- 1/4 teaspoon ground cinnamon
- 1 cup quick-cooking rice
- 1 egg, well beaten
- 1/8 teaspoon ground nutmeg
- Aresol whip cream if desired

Direction

- In a medium saucepan, combine all ingredients.
- Bring to a boil over medium heat.
- Cool for 5 minutes, stirring twice.
- Chill until serving.
- Top with whipped cream.

17. COCONUT RICE PUDDING ARROZ CON LECHE DE COCO Recipe

Serving: 8 | Prep: | Cook: 65mins | Ready in:

Ingredients

- This version is popular in Puerto Rico. To toast the coconut, spread it out on a baking sheet and toast it in a 325-degree oven, stirring often, until light golden, 10 to 15 minutes. We prefer pudding made from medium-grain rice, but long-grain rice works too. Using a heavy-bottomed saucepan here is key to prevent the bottom from burning.
- INGREDIENTS
- 2 cups water
- 1 cup medium-grain rice
- 1/4 teaspoon salt
- 2 1/2 cups coconut milk
- 2 1/2 cups half-and-half
- 2/3 cup sugar (4 2/3 ounces)
- 1/2 cup raisins
- 1 1/2 teaspoons vanilla extract
- 1 teaspoon ground cinnamon
- 1 cup sweetened shredded coconut , toasted (see note)

Direction

- INSTRUCTIONS
- 1. Bring the water to a boil in a large, heavy-bottomed saucepan. Stir in the rice and salt, cover, and simmer over low heat, stirring once or twice, until the water is almost fully absorbed, 15 to 20 minutes.
- 2. Stir in the coconut milk, half-and-half, and sugar. Increase the heat to medium-high and bring to a simmer, then reduce the heat to maintain a simmer. Cook, uncovered and stirring frequently, until the mixture starts to thicken, about 30 minutes. Reduce the heat to low and continue to cook, stirring every

couple of minutes to prevent sticking and scorching, until a spoon is just able to stand up in the pudding, about 15 minutes longer.
- 3. Remove from the heat and stir in the raisins, vanilla, and cinnamon. Serve warm, at room temperature, or chilled. Sprinkle with toasted coconut before serving. (To store, press plastic wrap directly on the surface of the pudding and refrigerate for up to 2 days. If serving at room temperature or chilled, stir in up to 1 cup warm milk, 2 tablespoons at a time, as needed to loosen before serving.)

18. CREAMY RICE PUDDING Recipe

Serving: 68 | Prep: | Cook: 120mins | Ready in:

Ingredients

- 2/3 c. uncooked rice
- 2/3 c. sugar
- 2 qt. milk
- 1 tsp. salt
- 2 tsp. vanilla
- 1 can evaporated milk
- Sprinkles of nutmeg

Direction

- Bake in 350 degree oven for 2 hours, stirring occasionally first hour. 1/2 cup raisins may be added 1/2 hour before end of baking time if desired. Pudding thickens as it cools.

19. Campfire Rice Pudding Recipe

Serving: 15 | Prep: | Cook: 30mins | Ready in:

Ingredients

- 4 cups rice
- 6 eggs

- 6 cups sugar
- 4 cup milk
- vanilla
- cinnamon

Direction

- Put water in pot and all rice. Cook rice till done
- Drain most all the water off rice, leave just a little so it isn't sticky
- Add the other ingredients and stir and let cook till thickened.
- You can sprinkle with cinnamon if desired...cocoa is good too.

20. Caramel Rice Pudding Crockpot Recipe

Serving: 8 | Prep: | Cook: 40120mins | Ready in:

Ingredients

- 3 cups cooked white rice
- 1/2 cup dried cranberries or cherries
- 1 tsp pure vanilla
- 1 can (14 oz) sweetened condensed milk*
- 1 can (12 oz) evaporated milk*
- 1 TBS brown sugar
- 1 tsp cinnamon

Direction

- Spray inside of 2 to 3.5 quart crockpot with cooking spray (or grease with butter).
- Mix all ingredients except sugar and cinnamon in crock.
- Cover and cook on LOW 3 to 4 hours or until liquid is absorbed. Stir pudding. Sprinkle pudding with sugar and cinnamon. Serve warm.
- Makes 8 servings
- NOTE: Reduced fat sweetened condensed milk and skim (fat free) evaporative milk may also be used.

21. Caramel Rice Pudding Recipe

Serving: 8 | Prep: | Cook: 90mins | Ready in:

Ingredients

- 2/3 cup rice (arborio or carolina)
- 4 eggs
- 1 spoonfull margarine
- ¼ teaspoon salt
- 4 cups milk
- 4 - 6 tablespoons sugar
- For caramel sauce
- ¼ cup granulated sugar
- ½ teaspoon lemon juice
- Water

Direction

- Melt granulated sugar in small saucepan with lemon juice and water (enough to wet sugar) and stir until brown, but do not burn; pour it while hot into pudding mold and spread it with a spoon, all over inside.
- Wash rice, drain, and cook slowly in milk for 45 minutes; turn into basin, add butter, salt, and eggs well beaten with sugar, and pour into prepared mold.
- Set mold in bain marie (pan of boiling water) and bake in preheated oven at 180o C, till quite set (about 45 minutes).
- Turn out and serve hot or cold.

22. Carolina Gold Rice Pudding Recipe

Serving: 8 | Prep: | Cook: 50mins | Ready in:

Ingredients

- 1 cup short-grain white rice
- 1/2 teaspoon salt

- 1 can sweetened condensed milk - (14 oz)
- 4 tablespoons butter
- 1/2 cup raisins
- 1 1/2 tablespoons vanilla extract
- 1 pinch freshly-grated nutmeg
- === fruit SAUCE ===
- 1 cup orange juice
- 1/2 cup sugar
- 1 tablespoon cornstarch
- 2 teaspoons fresh lemon juice
- 2 tablespoons butter
- 1/4 teaspoon rum extract - (to 1/2)
- 1 cup stewed fruit -- (optional)

Direction

- Put the rice in the top of a double boiler set over simmering water. Add the salt and 3 cups of boiling water. Cover and cook until the rice is tender, about 30 minutes.
- Stir in the condensed milk, butter, and raisins. Cook, stirring frequently, over simmering water until the pudding thickens slightly, about 20 minutes.
- Remove the pot from the heat and stir in the vanilla and nutmeg. Spoon the pudding into individual custard cups and refrigerate until ready to serve. Invert puddings onto chilled plates and serve with fruit sauce.
- Fruit Sauce: Combine the orange juice, sugar, and cornstarch in the top of a double boiler. Cook the mixture over simmering water until it thickens.
- Remove the pot from the heat and stir in the lemon juice, butter, and rum extract. Serve warm over rice pudding garnished with stewed fruit, if desired. (Makes about 1 1/2 cups)

23. Chai Tea Rice Pudding Recipe

Serving: 10 | Prep: | Cook: 20mins | Ready in:

Ingredients

- 8 Ounces whole milk
- 8 Ounces Chai tea Mixture (see recipe below)
- 8 ounces Risotto (Arborio) rice
- 1 quart plain yogurt
- Mix tea and milk together and bring to a boil. Add rice and cook until soft. Cool and fold in yogurt.

Direction

- Chai Tea Mixture
- 2 each Cardamom Pods, crushed lightly
- 1 ounce Cinnamon Sticks, crushed lightly
- 1 teaspoon black peppercorns, whole
- 1 ounce Brown Sugar
- 1 ounce Vanilla Bean Puree
- 1 teaspoon Earl Grey Tea, loose
- 8 ounces water
- Mix all ingredients together and bring to a boil. Let steep for one hour. Strain and cool.

24. Chocolate Almond Brown Rice Pudding Recipe

Serving: 8 | Prep: | Cook: 40mins | Ready in:

Ingredients

- 1 cup short or medium grain brown rice
- pinch of salt
- 1 2/3 cup water
- 3 tbsp. cocoa powder
- 1/4 tsp cinnamon
- 1 pkg. (946 ml) almond milk
- 1/2 cup white sugar
- 4 oz. bittersweet chocolate (85% cocoa solids) chopped
- 1/2 cup toasted sliced or slivered almonds

Direction

- In saucepan, combine rice, salt and 1 2/3 cups water to a boil; immediately reduce heat to low, cover and simmer until liquid is absorbed, 25 to 30 minutes.

- While the rice is simmering whisk together cocoa, cinnamon and some of the almond milk until smooth; whisk in remaining almond milk.
- Stir this into the rice; increase heat and bring to simmer. Stir in sugar; simmer, stirring often, until rice is completely soft and pudding is thick and creamy, 35 to 45 minutes.
- Remove from heat and stir in chocolate until melted and well mixed.
- Serve warm or at room temperature. Sprinkle with almonds.
- Makes 8 servings

25. Christmas Rice Pudding Recipe

Serving: 6 | Prep: | Cook: | Ready in:

Ingredients

- 1-3/4 cups uncooked long grain rice
- 2 cups water
- 4 cups milk
- 1-1/2 cups sugar
- 1 teaspoon salt
- 1/4 cup butter or margarine
- sliced almonds and ground cinnamon, optional

Direction

- In a saucepan, combine the rice and water.
- Simmer for 10 minutes; add milk and bring to a boil.
- Reduce heat and simmer, uncovered, for 60-70 minutes or until rice is tender.
- Add sugar, salt and butter; mix well.
- Spoon into small bowls or dessert dishes.
- Garnish with almonds and sprinkle with cinnamon if desired.
- Yield: 6-8 servings.

26. Cinnamon Rice Pudding Recipe

Serving: 12 | Prep: | Cook: | Ready in:

Ingredients

- 3 qts of milk
- 2 tbsp cinnamon, ground
- 1/4 cup of butter
- 2 cups sugar (white)
- 1 cup of heavy cream
- 4 eggs
- 1 cup white rice, uncooked

Direction

- In a large pot, mix the rice, butter, milk and cinnamon. Once at a boil, reduce the heat to low, and simmer for 30 minutes (until the rice is tender). Now, slowly add in the sugar. Whisk together the eggs and heavy cream in a medium sized bowl, until smooth. Gradually stir in around a cup of the hot milk mixture, (enough to raise the temperature slightly above body temperature). Slowly add the warmed egg mixture to the pot. (This will avoid the egg from scrambling). Simmer the pudding over low heat for around 10 minutes, constantly stirring until it has thickened. Then, pour the pudding into a bowl or baking dish. Allow the pudding to cool for 10-15 minutes before putting it in the refrigerator, then refrigerate for at least 2 hours before serving.

27. Coconut Brown Rice Pudding Recipe

Serving: 10 | Prep: | Cook: 60mins | Ready in:

Ingredients

- ½ cup brown rice (preferably short grain)
- ½ cup Unsweetened shredded coconut (optional)
- 1 can light coconut milk

- 1 cup   rice milk (preferably unsweetened)
- ¼ cup honey (locally made is best)
- 1 tsp   cinnamon
- 1 tsp   ginger
- 1 tsp vanilla extract
- ½ tsp stevia (optional)
- Dash sea salt (optional)

Direction

- Put all your ingredients into a medium saucepan and bring to a boil over medium-high heat.
- As soon as you begin to see bubbles coming to the top, reduce your heat to low and stir until the liquid is gently simmering.
- Cook uncovered for 1 hour. Stir with a whisk every 10-15 minutes.
- After an hour, most of the liquid will be absorbed by the rice, and the rice will have a tender but chewy texture.
- In the warmer months, you can allow the pudding to cool and then chill it in the refrigerator for at least an hour. When you're ready to serve, just spoon it into a bowl or parfait dish and top with fresh fruit like bananas, peaches or pineapple.
- In the cooler months of the year, I prefer to serve the pudding straight off the stove with raisins or dried cranberries. You can even add these in for the last 15 minutes of cooking time if you like them plump and juicy.
- Notes about ingredients:
- • Short grain brown rice has a better look and texture than long grain for pudding, and it has the same health benefits—high in fiber, vitamins, and minerals.
- • Coconut milk contains saturated fat, but the short-and medium-chain fatty acids of coconut milk are easily and quickly assimilated by the body. Unlike the long chain fats of animal products, they are not as likely to be stored as fat in the body. And light coconut milk has much less fat than regular coconut milk.
- • Unsweetened organic rice milk is a low-sugar, high nutrient alternative to regular milk, but almond and soy milk are healthy choices, too.
- • Local honey is usually fresher and can help you with seasonal allergies.
- • Cinnamon is great for blood sugar regulation, so feel free to add more if you enjoy a stronger cinnamon flavor.
- • Ginger is great for your digestion, so adding it to desserts is a good idea.
- • Stevia is an all-natural sweetener with no calories.
- • Sea Salt has a more robust flavor than regular salt, so you don't need much of it.

28. Coconut Date Rice Pudding Recipe

Serving: 10 | Prep: | Cook: 25mins |Ready in:

Ingredients

- 1 cup white rice
- 2 cups water
- 3/4 cup sugar
- 3/4 cup dried dates, chopped
- 1-1/3 cup coconut milk
- 1 cup shredded sweetened coconut
- 1/8 teaspoon allspice

Direction

- 1. Bring rice and water to a boil, turn down to low heat and cover, simmer for 15 minutes. (You can add a bit more water if it all cooks out before the time is up)
- 2. Add sugar, coconut milk, and dates. Stir together, then cook over low heat until most of liquid is absorbed, about 10 minutes.
- 3. Add shredded coconut and allspice and remove from heat. Let cool and refrigerate. Serve cold for dessert, snacks, or a delicious breakfast.
- Makes about 5 cups

29. Coconut Lime Rice Pudding Recipe

Serving: 4 | Prep: | Cook: 25mins | Ready in:

Ingredients

- 1/2 c jasmine rice
- 1 14oz can coconut milk
- 1 1/4 c whole milk
- 1/2 c sugar
- 1 1/2 to 2 t finely grated lime zest
- toasted coconut and/or lime wedges for garnish

Direction

- In a bowl soak rice in cold water to cover for 30 minutes. Drain rice in a sieve. In a heavy saucepan bring coconut milk, whole milk, rice, sugar and a pinch of salt to a boil and gently simmer, uncovered, stirring occasionally about 25 minutes. Remove from heat.
- Stir lime zest into pudding. Pudding may be made 2 days ahead and chilled, covered.
- Serve warm or chilled, garnish with coconut and lime
- For an elegant presentation make pudding shells by placing won ton wraps in muffin tins brushed with butter, bake shells until lightly browned, about 5 to 6 min. Scoop rice pudding into shells, top with mango slices and toasted coconut.

30. Coconut Rice Pudding Recipe

Serving: 8 | Prep: | Cook: 40mins | Ready in:

Ingredients

- • 1 1/2 cups cooked rice (unsalted, cold and cooked with one stick of cinnamon and half a lemon zest and 2 tspoons of vanilla stract)…Use four cups of water to cook it.
- • 1 can of condensed milk
- • 1 can of evaporated milk (You can use low fat)
- • 1 cup of whole milk
- • 1/2 cup coconut milk (unsweetened)
- • 1 1/2 teaspoon coconut extract
- • toasted coconut flakes for garnish

Direction

- 1. Place cooked rice, condensed milk, evaporated milk, whole milk, and coconut milk, in a pot.
- 2. Bring to a simmer, covered over moderate heat.
- 3. Simmer until the pudding has thickened; approximately 45 minutes. Stir frequently.
- 4. Add coconut extract and let simmer for one more minute. You can serve it cold or warm.

31. Coconutty Rice Pudding With Golden Raisins Recipe

Serving: 6 | Prep: | Cook: 20mins | Ready in:

Ingredients

- 1 c cooked basmati rice
- 1 c milk
- 1/2 c heavy cream
- 3/4 c coconut milk
- 1/4 c sugar
- 1/4 t ground cardamom
- 1/3 c golden raisins
- 2 oz Malibu rum
- toasted coconut

Direction

- In small bowl combine rum and raisins, microwave for about a minute or till raisins begin to plump. Cool.
- In large saucepan combine the cooked rice and milk and cook over med. heat till mixture begins to boil. Decrease heat to low and

simmer until mixture begins to thicken, stirring often, approximately 5 minutes.

- Increase heat to medium, add the heavy cream, coconut milk, sugar and cardamom and continue to cook until the mixture just begins to thicken approx. 5 to 10 minutes. When mixture thickens, remove from heat and stir in drained raisins and toasted coconut. Pour into individual serving dishes and place plastic wrap on surface of the pudding.

32. Creamiest Rice Pudding Recipe

Serving: 1 | Prep: | Cook: 75mins | Ready in:

Ingredients

- 1/2 gallon milk
- 1 cup white sugar
- 1 cup uncooked long-grain white rice
- 3 eggs, lightly beaten
- 1/4 cup milk
- 1/4 teaspoon salt
- 2 teaspoons vanilla extract
- ground cinnamon to taste

Direction

- In a large saucepan over medium-low heat, combine 1/2 gallon milk, sugar and rice. Simmer, Covered, 1 hour, stirring frequently. Remove pan from heat and let rest 10 minutes.
- In a small bowl, combine eggs, 1/4 cup milk, salt and vanilla. Stir into rice mixture and Return pot to low heat, stirring constantly, for 2 minutes.
- Pour into a 9x13 inch dish and Cover with plastic wrap, folding back the corners to allow the steam to escape.
- When pudding has cooled to room temperature, remove plastic wrap and sprinkle surface of Pudding with cinnamon. Cover tightly (with fresh wrap) and refrigerate 8 or overnight.

33. Creamy No Bake Rice Pudding Recipe

Serving: 6 | Prep: | Cook: 70mins | Ready in:

Ingredients

- 2 cups water
- 1 cup arborio rice
- 1/4 teasp salt
- 3 cups half and half --- OR
- I USE: 1 c. Soy milk, 1c. vanilla almond milk , 1 c. Half & Half
- 2 sticks of cinnamon
- 1 cup sugar
- 1 TBSP vanilla or to taste

Direction

- Bring 2 cups of water to a boil in a heavy non-stick pot that has a tight lid
- Add rice and the salt. Cover and lower the heat to simmer.
- Cook 20 mins.
- Next add 3 cups of whatever type of Milk you are using and the cinnamon sticks. Stir bring to a boil and then turn heat down to simmer.
- Simmer for 20 mins with the cover off.
- At the end of the 20 mins stir really well.
- Simmer for another 20 mins with the cover off.
- At the end of this 20 mins it should be getting thick it may need a little more time
- Next add the sugar. Mix well. It will look thin again that's okay.
- Simmer for another 10 or more mins or until it looks thick enough. It will thicken up more as it cools down. Take off the heat and add the Vanilla. Mix well. I usually add a little cinnamon powder... oh take the cinnamon sticks out.
- You will need to know your stove to get the temperatures right. So you may need a little more or less time cooking it

34. Creamy Pumpkin Rice Pudding Recipe

Serving: 6 | Prep: | Cook: 65mins | Ready in:

Ingredients

- 2/3 cup water
- 1/3 cup uncooked long grain rice
- 3 eggs, lightly beaten
- 1 cup milk
- 2/3 cup canned pumpkin
- 1/3 cup packed brown sugar
- 1 tsp pumpkin pie spice
- 1 tsp vanilla
- 1/4 tsp salt
- 3/4 cup dried cranberries or raisins
- 1 medium red apple and/or green pear, cored and thinly sliced (1 cup)
- 1/2 cup coarsely chopped walnuts, toasted
- 2 Tbsp honey

Direction

- Preheat oven to 325 degrees.
- In a small saucepan combine water and rice. Bring boiling; reduce heat. Simmer, covered, 15 minutes or until all liquid is absorbed, stirring once.
- In a medium bowl, combine eggs, milk, pumpkin, brown sugar, pie spice, vanilla, and salt.
- Stir in rice and 1/2 cup of the cranberries.
- Pour mixture into 1 1/2-quart straight-sided deep baking dish.
- Place dish in baking pan on oven rack. Pour boiling water into baking pan until water comes halfway up sides of baking dish.
- Bake 30 minutes; stir. Bake 35 minutes more or until outside edge appears set.
- Remove dish from oven and cool slightly on wire rack.
- Meanwhile, in a bowl combine remaining 1/4 cup cranberries and boiling water to cover. Let stand 15 minutes; drain.
- Just before serving, toss together apple, walnuts, honey and cranberries.
- Spoon over pudding. Serve warm.
- To store, cover and refrigerate for up to 24 hours.

35. Creamy Rice Apple Pud Recipe

Serving: 6 | Prep: | Cook: 45mins | Ready in:

Ingredients

- 3 cups skim milk
- 1 ½ cups water
- ¾ cup brown long-grain rice
- 2 tbsp brown sugar
- 1 large egg, beaten
- 1 tsp vanilla extract
- 1 tsp maple extract
- 1 medium macintosh apple, chopped

Direction

- In large saucepan, combine milk, water, rice and sugar.
- Bring rice to a boil over medium-high heat; reduce heat to medium and simmer, stirring occasionally, until rice is tender, about 40 minutes.
- Remove 1/2 cup rice mixture and mix with egg.
- Return to saucepan and add vanilla, maple and apple.
- Serve warm.

36. Creamy Rice Pudding Recipe

Serving: 6 | Prep: | Cook: 40mins | Ready in:

Ingredients

- 3 cups milk
- 3/4 cup long-grain rice

- 3 cups half and half
- 3/4 cup sugar
- 3 eggs
- 1 tsp. vanilla
- 1/2 cup or more raisins
- cinnamon and nutmeg to taste

Direction

- In a 3-quart saucepan, bring milk to a simmer. Add rice gradually so that milk doesn't stop simmering. Stir, cover and simmer about 30 minutes, or until rice is tender and milk is absorbed. Remove from heat, stir in half and half and sugar.
- In a small bowl, beat eggs well, then stir into rice mixture. Return to medium heat and, stirring constantly, cook until mixture thickens enough to coat a wooden spoon. Stir in vanilla and raisins, pour into a serving dish and sprinkle with cinnamon and nutmeg.

37. Crockpot Rice Pudding Recipe

Serving: 8 | Prep: | Cook: 240mins | Ready in:

Ingredients

- 2 qts. (8 cups) vanilla soy milk
- 1 cup uncooked rice
- 1 cup sugar
- 3 Tbsp. cold margarine
- Pinch of salt
- 1 tsp. vanilla
- 1/2 tsp. cinnamon
- 1/4 cup dried cranberries, cherries, raisins,,, (optional)
- 1/4 cup chopped, pecans, almonds, walnuts.....(optional)

Direction

- Combine all the ingredients in a crock pot. Cook on low for 3 to 4 hours, stirring every hour, until the desired consistency is reached.

38. Cuban Coconut Rice Pudding Recipe

Serving: 6 | Prep: | Cook: 30mins | Ready in:

Ingredients

- 3 cups water
- 1 cup short grain rice
- 4 whole cloves
- 1 (2 inch) piece of vanilla bean, split lengthwise
- 1 (2 inch) cinnamon stick
- 1 (14 oz) can fat free sweetened condensed milk
- 1/2 cup evaporated fat free milk
- 1/2 cup light coconut milk
- 1/2 cup golden raisins
- 1 Tbsp. chopped crystallized ginger
- 1 tspp. grated lemon rind
- Dash of salt
- 1/2 tsp. ground cinnamon (optional)

Direction

- Place water and rice in a large saucepan.
- Place cloves, vanilla and cinnamon on a double layer of cheesecloth.
- Gather edges of cheesecloth together; tie securely.
- Add to rice mixture.
- Bring to a simmer over medium heat, stirring frequently.
- Reduce heat to low; cook for 20 minutes or until rice is tender and liquid is almost absorbed.
- Stir in milks and raisins; cook for 10 minutes; stirring frequently.
- Stir in ginger, rind, and salt and cook for 5 minutes, stirring frequently.
- Remove cheesecloth with spices.
- Pour rice mix into a bowl or individualized bowls; cover surface of pudding with plastic wrap.

- Chill.
- Sprinkle with cinnamon if desired.

39. Custard Rice Pudding Recipe

Serving: 6 | Prep: | Cook: 60mins | Ready in:

Ingredients

- 2 large eggs
- 1/2 cup sugar
- 1 tsp. vanilla
- 2 cups milk
- 2 cups Precooked rice
- 1 tbsp. butter, melted
- 1/2 cup raisins (or more)
- nutmeg

Direction

- Preheat oven to about 325 degrees F.
- Combine eggs, sugar and vanilla.
- Add 1/2 cup milk and stir. Repeat adding milk and stirring four times till milk is used.
- Add cooled, melted butter.
- Pour mixture into rice. Add raisins.
- Sprinkle nutmeg on top.
- Bake 1 hour or until knife inserted into middle comes out clean.

40. Date Rice Pudding Recipe

Serving: 8 | Prep: | Cook: 30mins | Ready in:

Ingredients

- 2 cups milk
- 2 cups cream
- 2 cups half and half
- 1 cup sugar
- 1 cup long grain rice
- 1 vanilla bean
- 2 Tbs rum

- dash salt
- 8 oz Pkg bite size chopped pitted dates
- 8 oz whipped topping or 1 cup cream whipped

Direction

- In heavy duty sauce pot heat milks, sugar, vanilla bean (split) over medium heat, stirring occasionally until mixture comes to a boil.
- Add rice and bring to a boil again.
- Reduce heat to a gentle simmer and cover and cook mixture (stir occasionally) until rice mixture becomes creamy and liquids almost absorbed.
- Pudding will thicken with chilling.
- Remove from heat, remove vanilla bean and stir in the dates.
- Let cool completely and then cover and chill very well.
- Then place mixture in a large glass or dessert bowl and blend in the whipped topping or the cream that has been whipped to lighten texture of the pudding. .
- Garnish pudding with chopped almonds and maraschino cherries if desired.
- Note: if you want date and nut rice pudding then blend in some slivered or sliced almonds along with the dates to the pudding instead of using as a garnish.
- For a lower calorie version one can make pudding with all milk or part milk and skim milk and use the whipped topping instead of the heavy cream.

41. Down South Rice Pudding Recipe

Serving: 6 | Prep: | Cook: 30mins | Ready in:

Ingredients

- 1 c. uncooked rice
- 1 c. water
- 3 -4 c. milk

- 1 tsp. salt
- 1/4 cup sugar
- 2 eggs, beaten (put in a bowl and set aside)
- Grated rind of 1/2 a lemon
- 1/3 c. raisins
- 1 tsp. vanilla extract
- Fine dried bread crumbs
- 1 T. butter

Direction

- Heat rice in water
- Add 3 cups of milk, salt and sugar
- Cover and simmer for 40 minutes or until rice is tender
- Add more milk if necessary to keep rice from becoming dry
- Stir frequently during cooking
- Remove from heat
- Add 1/2 cup of cooked rice to the beaten eggs
- Transfer rice/egg combo to the rest of the mixture
- Add lemon rind, raisins and vanilla
- Butter a 1 1/2 quart casserole dish (bottom and sides) and cover bottom and sides with bread crumbs
- Pour rice mixture into casserole
- Dot with butter and sprinkle with crumbs
- Place in a preheated 325 F oven for 30 minutes or until set
- Cool and unmold
- * For an added "sweet treat", serve with strawberries, raspberries or a stewed fruit

42. Easy Rice Pudding Recipe

Serving: 8 | Prep: | Cook: 35mins | Ready in:

Ingredients

- 4.5 cups milk (I use 1%)
- 1/3 cup sugar
- 3/4 cup cooked rice (a great way to use leftover rice! We use jasmine rice)
- 1 tsp vanilla

- 1/4 cup custard powder

Direction

- Bring milk and sugar to rolling boil in medium-large saucepan.
- Add rice and custard powder and turn heat to low.
- HERE is where you need patience. Keep boiling on low for 30 minutes!
- After 30 minutes, I normally turn it up to high again and rapidly boil the mixture for an added 5 minutes or so, but it is not necessary.
- Let sit for 5-10 minutes and serve.
- This is delicious hot or cold!!

43. English Baked Rice Pudding Recipe

Serving: 4 | Prep: | Cook: 120mins | Ready in:

Ingredients

- 5 cups milk
- 2 tbsp cream
- 1 cup shor grain rice
- 1 oz vanilla sugar (insert a vanilla bean pod into a jar of granulated sugar, screw on the lid)
- grated peel of 1/2 lemon
- 1/2 tsp nutmeg

Direction

- Heat the milk and cream but do not boil. Spray a casserole dish with cooking spray. Mix the rice with the milk and pour into the dish. Let stand for 20 minutes. Stir in the sugar and lemon peel and sprinkle the top with nutmeg. Bake in a preheated oven at 300 degrees for 2 hours. Stir well every half an hour.

44. English Rice Pudding Recipe

Serving: 6 | Prep: | Cook: 40120mins | Ready in:

Ingredients

- 2 litres milk
- 3 tablespoons rice
- 3 tablespoons sugar

Direction

- Preheat oven to 160C.
- Grease oven-proof dish.
- Combine milk, sugar, and rice in dish.
- Bake in oven for 3 to 4 hours (possibly even longer) stirring occasionally, until the pudding is thick and creamy.
- Serve warm or cold.

45. Fantastically Fruity Rice Pudding Recipe

Serving: 16 | Prep: | Cook: 3hours | Ready in:

Ingredients

- 3 cups cooked short grain rice
- 4 cups whole milk
- ½ cup sugar or stevia baking blend
- ½ tsp salt
- 2 eggs, beaten
- 1 cup frozen raspberries
- 1 tbsp vanilla

Direction

- Combine rice, milk, sugar and salt in a pot and cook over medium heat until thick, about 15 to 20 minutes.
- Stir in eggs and raspberries and cook 2 minutes more, stirring constantly.
- Remove from heat and stir in vanilla.

46. Firni Or Rice Flour Pudding Recipe

Serving: 8 | Prep: | Cook: 15mins | Ready in:

Ingredients

- 1 lr milk
- 1/2 C uncooked rice
- 1 1/2 C sugar
- 2 cardamoms
- 10 almonds
- 15 pistachios
- 1 tsp screwpine leaves (pandan) essence
- Edible silver leaves for garnishing

Direction

- Soak the rice for 3 hours.
- Drain water and dry thoroughly.
- Powder it using a mixer.
- Bring the milk to boil, stirring all the time.
- Add the sugar and rice.
- Stir for 15 mins until thickened.
- Remove from heat.
- Add the essence and the nuts
- Garnish and chill for 2 hrs. before serving

47. Fried Rice Pudding Won Tons In Mango Sauce Recipe

Serving: 6 | Prep: | Cook: 15mins | Ready in:

Ingredients

- 1 pint quality coconut ice cream
- 1 pint mango sorbet (recipe listed separately)
- 1 cup your favorite rice pudding (home-made or store bought)
- 24 Won Ton wrappers
- 1/2 cup mango chunks
- 1 Tbl. dark rum
- oil for deep frying
- mint sprigs for garnish

Direction

- Heat up oil in a deep fryer.
- Using to tablespoons, form the ice cream and sorbet into quenelles on a chilled pan, place pan with quenelles in freeze for later service.
- Place mango and rum into a blender and puree, set aside.
- Place a tablespoon of rice pudding in middle of a won ton wrapper and wet edge of wrapper with a finger dipped in water.
- Place a second wrapper on top of the first and gently seal won tons together removing as much air as possible from between the won tons.
- Place the filled won ton in the fryer and fry until golden brown, repeat this procedure for the other won tons and pudding.
- Place two fried won tons on each plate, along with one of each flavored quenelle.
- Drizzle mango sauce over the won tons, garnish each plate with a mint sprig and serve.
- Note: You can use any ice cream or sorbet you like with the won tons. I like just plain coconut ice cream and chocolate sauce. Get creative!

48. Ginger Infused Japanese Rice Pudding Recipe

Serving: 1034 | Prep: | Cook: 90mins | Ready in:

Ingredients

- syrup:
- 1/2 cup water
- 2/3 cup plus 2 tbsp brown sugar
- 1/2 cupc sugar
- pudding:
- 3 tbsp grated peeled fresh ginger
- 3 cups 1% low fat milk, divided
- 3 cups plain soy milk
- 1 cup short-grain rice
- 1/4 cup heavy cream
- 10 fresh strawberries, sliced
- crysallized ginger for garnish (optional)

Direction

- Syrup:
- In a medium saucepan, combine water and sugars. Cook over med heat until boiling.
- Turn heat to low and simmer about 30 minutes. Stir occasionally.
- Pudding:
- Place grated ginger in cheesecloth with a tie string.
- Combine milk, soymilk, and ginger tea bag in a large saucepan.
- Simmer over low heat for 15-20 minutes.
- Occasionally skim top.
- Remove ginger bag and stir in rice and syrup.
- Cook on high until mixture boils. Reduce heat to med-low and simmer uncovered, stirring often until pudding thickens and rice is tender (about 45 minutes) then add heavy cream.
- Spoon pudding into serving cups and top each one with a strawberry and the ginger if using.

49. Grandma's Best Rice Pudding Recipe

Serving: 4 | Prep: | Cook: 2hours | Ready in:

Ingredients

- 1/3 cup (80 mL) Arborio (short-grain Italian) rice
- 2 cups (500 mL) Milk
- 3 tbsp (45 mL) sugar
- 3 tbsp (45 mL) butter softened
- Grated zest of 1 lemon
- 1 tsp (5 mL) ground cinnamon

Direction

- Preheat the oven to 250° F (120 °C).
- Mix the rice, milk, sugar, butter and lemon zest together in a bowl and pour the mixture

into a buttered 8-cup (2 L) baking dish. Bake uncovered for 2 hrs.

- Sprinkle with cinnamon and serve hot or cold.

50. Greek Diner Rice Pudding Recipe

Serving: 810 | Prep: | Cook: 20mins | Ready in:

Ingredients

- 2 cups carolina rice or similar
- 2 quarts milk
- 1 whole lemon peel
- ~~~~~~~~~~~~~~~~~~~~~~~~~~~
- 6 large eggs
- 2 cups cane sugar (can be substituted with splenda- 1/4 cup or according to your taste)
- 1 teaspoon vanilla
- ~~~~~~~~~~~~~~~~~~~~~~~~~~~
- 2 cups heavy cream
- ~~~~~~~~~~~~~~~~~~~~~~~~~~~
- Sprinkle cinnamon

Direction

- *Place milk, rice and lemon peel into sauce pot- bring to a boil then adjust temperature to simmer for approximately 20 minutes. Stirring constantly to avoid sticking and scorching.
- *Hand mix the eggs, sugar and vanilla together.
- *Remove the lemon peel and discard only after the rice has plumped. (Rice will seem to be over cooked)
- *When the rice is cooked correctly remove from the heat and add the egg, sugar and vanilla mixture slowly, stirring constantly. This mixture will thicken. Be sure to blend this mixture thoroughly. Taste with a spoon.
- *Chill your rice pudding into a glass bowl. Chill for 1 hour.
- *Whip the heavy cream till just before soft peaks.

- *Fold cream into the rice pudding mixture. Taste with a spoon. Sprinkle with ground cinnamon. Taste with a spoon, Cover and refrigerate.
- * Always taste and ENJOY.

51. Holiday Rice Pudding Recipe

Serving: 68 | Prep: | Cook: 15mins | Ready in:

Ingredients

- 3 cups cooked rice
- 3 cups milk
- 1/2 cup sugar
- 3 tablespoons butter or margarine
- 1/2 cup dried cranberries
- Finely grated zest of 1 lemon
- 1 teaspoon vanilla extract

Direction

- Combine rice, milk, sugar and butter in 2- to 3-quart saucepan. Cook over medium heat, stirring often, 20 minutes. Add cranberries and lemon rind; cook 10 minutes. Remove from heat; add vanilla. Spoon into serving dishes.
- Makes 6 servings.

52. Hunts Family Rice Pudding Recipe

Serving: 12 | Prep: | Cook: 60mins | Ready in:

Ingredients

- 6 cups milk
- ¾ cup long rice pudding
- 1 cup heavy cream
- ¾ cup sugar
- 3 egg yolks beaten
- 2 teaspoons vanilla
- ¼ teaspoon salt

- Optional: last 15 minutes of cooking you can add raisins. I pre soak them in water or sometimes rum and drain the liquid before adding.
- 1 teaspoon cinnamon

Direction

- Rinse pan with cold water and do not dry.
- Pour milk in and bring to a boil.
- Stir in rice and return to a boil.
- Reduce heat and simmer, uncovered until rice is tender for about 55 minutes.
- Stir occasionally.
- Meanwhile combine cream sugar, egg yolks, vanilla, and salt and set aside.
- When the rice is tender, stir in cream mixture until completely combined: heat to a boil. (I usually add some hot liquid to the cream mixture first to temper it, then add it to the pot)
- Remove from heat and pour into a 2 quart dish.
- Sprinkle top generously with cinnamon.
- Chill at least 4 hours.
- Optional: Top it off with homemade whip cream. ONLY homemade whip cream.
- This makes 6 cups.
- I usually double this. Believe me it goes.
- This is the best rice pudding. I was never a fan until I started eating this.

53. Imbolc Milk And Honey Rice Pudding Recipe

Serving: 4 | Prep: | Cook: 60mins | Ready in:

Ingredients

- Pudding:
- 3 eggs beaten gently
- 1c milk
- ½ c sweetened condensed milk
- 1/3 c honey
- 1 tsp vanilla

- 1 c cooked
- ***88
- rice Sauce:
- Equal Parts sweetened condensed milk and honey
- cinnamon (optional)

Direction

- In a mixing bowl combine eggs, milk, condensed milk, honey and vanilla.
- Beat gently by hand until honey is dissolved.
- Stir in rice.
- Pour into a 1.5 quart baking dish.
- Place the baking dish into a larger baking dish and put 1 inch of hot water into the outer dish.
- Bake for 45-60 minutes or until a knife inserted into the center comes out clean.
- Remove immediately from the hot water bath.
- Set aside while you make the sauce.
- In a glass bowl mix equal parts condensed milk and honey.
- Heat in the microwave in 10 second intervals and stir until well mixed.
- Stir in cinnamon to taste.
- Drizzle over individual servings of warm pudding.

54. Indian Rice Pudding (Kheer) Recipe

Serving: 2 | Prep: | Cook: 30mins | Ready in:

Ingredients

- 1 litre of full fat milk
- 1/2 small tea cup of long grain rice soaked for atleast 1 hour
- 1 cup of sugar (u can use as much sweet u want)
- 1 tsp of cardamon powder or vanilla
- few strands of saffron
- some nuts to decorate (opt)

Direction

- In a deep pan boil the milk give it one boil n add the rice. Now start stirring with a wooden spoon, keep stirring in a high to medium heat. Milk and rice will start cooking together
- Add vanilla/cardamom powder (I prefer cardamom powder) after 10 min add sugar and saffron
- Cook till milk reduces in to half. In between cooking take a spoon or spatula and scrap out the line create by milk around the pot this is milk cream which thickens the pudding
- Mix it in the pudding, keep stirring
- In 25 mins u will see rice is cooked in the milk and milk has thicken up like a cream
- Close the stove cover the lid n let it rest. Cool it down completely and serve with nuts. Ready to eat!!!!
- Tip: Always use wooden spoon, as while stirring helps rice to release starch
- For rice pudding use full fat milk no skimmed milk will give the effect of the pudding.
- After all once in a while we should treat ourselves
- Enjoy!!!!! :-)

55. Indian Rice Pudding Kheer Recipe

Serving: 8 | Prep: | Cook: 45mins | Ready in:

Ingredients

- 5 C whole milk (approximate)
- 1/4 C sugar (more to taste, if desired - I prefer dishes to be less sweet)
- 3 green cardamom pods, seeds extracted and ground, or 1/2 tsp ground cardamom (optional)
- 1 C basmati rice
- 2 Tbsp ghee (clarified butter) or unsalted butter
- crushed almonds (optional)

Direction

- In a saucepan, warm milk. Dissolve sugar in it, and remove from heat. Stir in ground cardamom.
- Sauté the rice in butter until it turns translucent, approximately 2 minutes over medium-high heat.
- Turn the heat down to medium-low. By 1/2 cups, add the milk, stirring until it is absorbed. As the rice cooks, it will take longer and longer for the milk to be absorbed.
- If the rice grains are not tender by the time the milk is gone, add more milk and continue process under they are. (It's OK to add it straight from the carton.)
- Adjust sweetening to taste.
- Serve warm or cold, garnished with a spoonful of crushed almonds, if desired.

56. Indian Rice Pudding Or Kheer Recipe

Serving: 12 | Prep: | Cook: 45mins | Ready in:

Ingredients

- rice – 1 cup (I use Basmati)
- milk – 2 litres (full cream)
- cardamom – 5-6 (seeds ground in pestle & mortar)
- saffron strands – 1 pinch (soaked for 10 mins in 1 tbsp warm milk)
- raisins – ¼ cup
- almonds – ¼ cup
- sugar – ¾ cup (Start with ½ cup and increase if required)
- Cream – ½ cup (optional for a GREATER tasting kheer/pudding)
- Nutmeg- 1/2 tsp grated fresh

Direction

- Put the milk (less ½ cup) in a heavy bottom pan and bring to a boil, stirring often.
- Blanch the almonds in boiling water for 2-3 minutes and peel them. Reserve for later.

- Meanwhile, wash rice, drain and microwave for 1 min. Separate the grains and microwave further for a minute.
- Spread out in a platter to cool, and then grind in a coffee grinder till nicely done. Set aside. (Can be done days in advance)
- Once the milk comes to a boil, mix the ground rice into the remaining cold ½ cup of milk.
- Stir this into the boiling milk, giving it a good stir since rice tends to form lumps otherwise.
- Add cardamom powder and saffron strands.
- Reduce heat to a simmer, add cream (YES, good idea!!), and allow to cook for about 45 mins till rice gets cooked and the kheer/pudding thickens to a good consistency. Make sure the milk is stirred on and off to avoid it becoming lumpy.
- Add the raisins, nutmeg and almonds (reserve a few almonds to slice for garnishing if desired).
- Add the sugar, mix well, adjust for sweetness, remove and allow it to cool.
- Once it cools down a bit, transfer to a bowl (or individual bowls) to set. Garnish if desired.
- Chill well (4-6 hours) before serving.
- Note: Varieties of rice differ…one kind may have more starch than the other.
- If you want it thicker (or if it doesn't thicken enough), add a tsp. of cornflour dissolved in 2 tbsp. of cold milk once the rice is cooked.
- Do remember though that the kheer/pudding will continue to thicken as it cools once done.
- Also if the kheer/pudding does appear lumpy after the rice is cooked, run the hand mixer/whisk through the kheer/pudding before the raisins and almonds are added!!

57. Indian Spiced Rice Pudding Recipe

Serving: 6 | Prep: | Cook: 30mins | Ready in:

Ingredients

- 1 3/4 cups water
- 1/2 cup jasmine or other white rice
- 14 oz can sweetened condensed milk
- 1 tsp vanilla
- 1 tsp cardamom
- 1 tsp mace blades (or 1/4 - 1/2 tsp ground mace)
- 1 cinnamon stick
- salt, to taste (I used 1/4 tsp)

Direction

- In a medium saucepan bring water, rice, cardamom, mace, cinnamon and salt to a boil. Reduce heat and simmer for 20-25 minutes, making sure rice doesn't stick.
- Add condensed milk and vanilla and cook another 5 minutes, stirring constantly. Remove cinnamon stick.
- Serve warm or cold. Will thicken as it cools.

58. Jeremys Mums Rice Pudding Recipe

Serving: 4 | Prep: | Cook: 90mins | Ready in:

Ingredients

- 1/2 cup rice
- 1/4 cup sugar
- 2 1/2 cups milk
- few shakes nutmeg
- few dots butter (i argue that the butter is unneccessary, but they tell me its what makes the crispy-like skin on top. Bah-humbug to butter, says Zoe the Unicorn)

Direction

- Put everything in an oven-proof dish and bake at 160C for an hour and a half.
- Serve by its self or ice cream and fruit.

59. KOZY SHACK RICE PUDDING Recipe

Serving: 8 | Prep: | Cook: 30mins | Ready in:

Ingredients

- 2 cups of water
- 1/2 tsp salt
- 1 cup uncooked regular white rice, medium grain (not parboiled)
- 4 cups heavy cream
- 5 extra-large eggs
- 1 cup sugar
- 1 tbl. pure vanilla extract

Direction

- Bring the water and salt to a boil in a large saucepan over high heat. Stir in the rice and return to a boil. Cover the pot, reduce the heat to low, and cook until all of the water is absorbed, about 20 minutes. Check the pot occasionally and stir to prevent the rice from sticking.
- Slowly stir 3 1/2 cups of the cream into the rice and stir gently over low heat until the cream is incorporated (make sure it does not boil). Remove the pan from the heat.
- Whip the eggs and sugar with an electric mixer on high until light yellow and thick. Beat a little hot cream into the eggs, then stir this egg mixture into the rice until it's blended throughout.
- Return the pudding to the heat and stir gently until it has thickened. It's very important not to let the mixture boil at this stage, as excess heat can curdle the eggs.
- Remove the pudding from the heat and immediately stir in the remaining 1/2 cup of cream and the vanilla. Transfer the pudding to a heatproof bowl and let it cool at room temperature for 30 minutes. Lay a piece of plastic wrap directly on the surface (this prevents a skin from forming on top) and refrigerate the pudding until it's cold. Store any leftovers in the refrigerator.

60. Kheer Rice Pudding Recipe

Serving: 2 | Prep: | Cook: 40mins | Ready in:

Ingredients

- 1/8 cup rice
- 1 1/4 cup milk
- 2 tbsp white sugar
- 1 cardamom pod
- raisins, nuts

Direction

- Wash the rice until water becomes clear. Put in a pot.
- Pour half of milk and mix. Cover with a lid and boil for 15-20 minutes until ready. Mash it.
- Add sugar and remaining milk. Heat for 10 minutes over low heat until it starts thicken.
- Add cardamom and raisins. Take the pot off the stove and pour into serving bowls.
- Decorate with nuts and raisins.
- Can be served hot or chilled.

61. LEFTOVER RICE PUDDING Recipe

Serving: 6 | Prep: | Cook: 25mins | Ready in:

Ingredients

- 3 cups cooked white rice
- 2 Tablespoons butter
- 4 cups milk
- 1/2 cup granulated sugar
- cinnamon, to taste (start with 1/2 teaspoon and go from there)
- 1 teaspoon vanilla
- 1 cup raisins (optional)

Direction

- In a large saucepan, stir together rice, butter, milk, sugar, cinnamon, vanilla, and raisins. Bring mixture to a boil over medium-high heat. Reduce heat to low and simmer 20-25 mins, stirring often (pudding will still be somewhat soupy, but will thicken in the refrigerator). Remove from heat and pour into large serving bowl. Cover with plastic wrap placed directly on the surface to prevent a "skin" from forming. Cool to room temperature before serving or refrigerating. Serve warm or cold. Store, covered, in the refrigerator.
- Note: Mixing the cinnamon and sugar together (like cinnamon/sugar) before adding to the rice mixture will make it easier to blend in. Adding the cinnamon by itself tends to make it clump a bit and it doesn't blend in as well. Recipe is easily halved.

62. Lebanese Rice Pudding Recipe

Serving: 8 | Prep: | Cook: 20mins | Ready in:

Ingredients

- 4C milk
- 1/4C powdered rice
- 3/4C water
- 1/2C-3/4C sugar (depending on how sweet you want it)
- 1/4C unsalted chopped nuts

Direction

- Mix rice with water and add to milk, which has been brought to a boil. Stir and cook until thickened and then add sugar. Continue cooking and stirring until mixture coats the spoon. Pour into individual serving dishes and decorate with chopped nuts.

63. Leftover Rice Pudding

Serving: 0 | Prep: | Cook: | Ready in:

Ingredients

- 2 cups cooked long grain rice
- 2 cups whole milk
- 3 tablespoons plus 1 teaspoon sugar
- 1/8 teaspoon salt
- 1 teaspoon vanilla extract
- Optional: whipped cream, cinnamon and dried cranberries

Direction

- In a large saucepan, combine the rice, milk, sugar and salt. Cook, uncovered, over medium heat until thickened, stirring often, about 20 minutes. Remove from the heat; stir in vanilla. Spoon into serving dishes. Serve warm. If desired, top with whipped cream, cinnamon and dried cranberries.
- Leftover Rice Pudding Tips
- How do you thicken rice pudding?
- Rice pudding will thicken as it cools, but if you prefer your pudding thicker, you can whisk in a beaten egg while the pudding is warming and continue cooking until it's thickened. To thicken cooled, cooked rice pudding, fold in whipped cream.
- Where was rice pudding invented?
- Rice pudding originated in England in the late 1300's and was primarily made for the elite classes because rice was an expensive import. At first, rice pudding was created as a savory side dish, similar to what we know as risotto today. In recent years, rice pudding has fallen back into favor as a classic, nostalgic dessert and it's a bit sweeter, too.
- What else can I do with leftover rice?
- Cooked white rice can be stored in an airtight container in the refrigerator for four to six days and used in a variety of dishes. Some of our favorites are fried rice, omelets> or any of these other white rice recipes.
- Nutrition Facts

- 2/3 cup: 221 calories, 4g fat (2g saturated fat), 12mg cholesterol, 127mg sodium, 39g carbohydrate (17g sugars, 0 fiber), 6g protein.

64. Lemon Poppy Seed Rice Pudding Recipe

Serving: 12 | Prep: | Cook: 70mins | Ready in:

Ingredients

- 3 quarts of whole milk
- 1 lb of arborio rice (Risotto quality rice) Avoid instant rice - it will ruin it!
- 1 14oz can of unsweetened coconut milk
- 1 whole vanilla bean, split and seeds scraped
- 2 Tbsp poppy-seeds
- 1 1/2 cups of sugar
- 1/2 cups of heavy or whipping cream
- Zest of one lemon

Direction

- 1. In a large, heavy pot, combine milk, rice, coconut milk. Mix well and let sit for 30 minutes. Add vanilla bean (entire bean and scraped seeds) and poppy seeds. Mix well and bring to a simmer over a moderately high heat. When it starts to bubble, reduce heat to low and simmer, stirring often, until the rice is tender (approximately 50-75 minutes).
- 2. Add the sugar, cream, and lemon zest and continue to simmer for another 10 minutes. Let cool to room temperature and cover with plastic wrap. Store in the refrigerator for at least 2 hours.

65. Lourdes Lemon Cinnamon Rice Pudding Recipe

Serving: 4 | Prep: | Cook: 20mins | Ready in:

Ingredients

- 1/2 C Valencia rice
- 4/5th C water
- pinch salt
- piece of lemon rind
- 1 cinnamon stick
- 1 can sweetened condensed milk
- 1 can evaporated milk
- 1 can coconut milk
- 1 tsp vanilla extract

Direction

- Boil water, place rice in boiling water. Bring to med/low setting, add lemon, cinnamon, salt and continue stirring. Add more water if necessary. You will end up with sticky, soupy rice (not runny). Add the three cans of milk and bring to a boil, then lower heat to med/low and add vanilla extract. Continue to stir until it becomes creamy.

66. Maple Rice Pudding Recipe

Serving: 4 | Prep: | Cook: 180mins | Ready in:

Ingredients

- 4 cups (1 L) milk
- 1/2 cup (125 ml) uncooked rice
- 1/3 cup (80 ml) pure maple syrup
- A pinch of salt
- 1/4 tsp (1 ml) almond extract
- 3 Tbs (45 ml) butter, melted

Direction

- Combine all ingredients except the butter in a baking dish.
- Bake at 250F (120C) for 1 hour, stirring every 15 minutes.
- Stir in the melted butter and continue cooking without stirring for an additional 2 hours.
- Serve warm, chilled, or at room temperature.
- Dollop of whipped cream of course!

- Serves 4 to 6.

67. Milchreis Recipe

Serving: 4 | Prep: | Cook: 10mins | Ready in:

Ingredients

- 1 cup of short grain rice (milchreis rice is best)
- 4 cups of milk (whole milk is best)
- 1/2 cup of brown sugar
- 1 stick of vanilla
- Some cinnamon to sprinkle or fruit to spread on top

Direction

- Mix all the ingredients together and bring to a boil. Let it simmer until the rice is sticky.
- Add cinnamon or fruit on top and serve lukewarm.

68. Minute Rice Pudding Recipe

Serving: 6 | Prep: | Cook: 15mins | Ready in:

Ingredients

- 5 cups whole milk
- 1 1/3 cups Minute Rice
- 1/2 cup sugar
- 1/4 teaspoon salt
- 2 tablespoons butter
- 1/2 teaspoon nutmeg (or more!)
- 2 teaspoons vanilla extract
- 1/2 cup raisins (optional)
- 2 eggs
- 2 tablespoons milk

Direction

- Bring to a boil the milk, rice, sugar, salt, butter, nutmeg, vanilla extract and raisins (If desired).

- Stir often.
- Beat together the 2 eggs and the 2 tablespoons milk.
- Slowly add the egg mixture to the rice, whisking constantly and rapidly.
- Remove from heat.
- Pour into serving or individual dishes.
- Top with whipped cream.
- Sprinkle with cinnamon, if desired.

69. Mommas Rice Pudding Old Recipe

Serving: 46 | Prep: | Cook: 60mins | Ready in:

Ingredients

- rice Pudding
- * 1/3 cup rice
- * 1/4 tsp salt
- * 4 Tbsp sugar
- * 4 cups milk (your choice of 1% or whole or 1/2 cream)
- * 1/4 tes. cinnamon

Direction

- Wash rice and place in baking dish. Add sugar salt and milk. Stir to dissolve. Cook in 350 deg. F. oven for 1 hour until rice is done. Raisins may be added and nutmeg.

70. Moroccan Rice Pudding Recipe

Serving: 6 | Prep: | Cook: 35mins | Ready in:

Ingredients

- 3/4 cup arborio rice
- 1 1/2 cups water
- 1/4 teaspoon salt
- 2 tablespoons plus 1 teaspoon unsalted butter

- 2 1/2 cups whole milk
- 3/4 cup confectioners' sugar
- 1 tablespoon orange-flower water (optional)
- 1/2 cup blanched almonds

Direction

- In a fine-mesh sieve, rinse the rice under cold water until the water runs clear.
- Transfer the rice to a medium saucepan.
- Add the water and salt and bring to a boil.
- Add 2 tablespoons of the butter, cover and cook over low heat until the water is almost completely absorbed, about 15 minutes.
- Stir in the milk and sugar and bring to a boil over moderate heat.
- Cook, stirring occasionally, until the rice is tender, about 7 minutes.
- Stir in the orange-flower water and simmer for 1 minute.
- Transfer the rice pudding to a bowl and let cool; the pudding will firm up.
- Meanwhile, in a small skillet, melt the remaining 1 teaspoon of butter.
- Add the almonds and cook over moderately high heat, stirring, until golden, about 6 minutes.
- Transfer the almonds to a plate to cool. Sprinkle the almonds over the pudding and serve.
- Make Ahead:
- The rice pudding can be refrigerated overnight.
- Serve chilled or at room temperature

71. Mothers Traditional Rice Pudding Recipe

Serving: 4 | Prep: | Cook: 2mins | Ready in:

Ingredients

- Rice- ½ cup Preferably scented rice like basmati uncooked

- Milk- 2 lit milk (evaporated milk powder can also be dissolved and used.)
- Sugar- 1cup
- raisin - ½ cup
- Cashewnut-1/2 cup
- Cardamom- 4 nos
- Bay leaf - 2nos
- Desiccated coconut cut into small fine pcs
- Cherry – for garnishing

Direction

- Wash rice and Soak rice for 3omins or so.
- Drain rice just before adding in to milk
- Boil milk in low flame and let it thicken for some time.
- Add bay leaf.
- Add soaked rice when the volume of milk reduces almost half.
- Stir it so that it is not stuck to the bottom.
- When rice gets half cooked add raisin, cashew nut, coconut pcs, shelled cardamom seeds.
- Stir thoroughly.
- Add sugar when rice is almost cooked and stir it continuously so that sugar gets mixed.
- (Don't add sugar before rice is cooked otherwise rice will remain uncooked!!)
- When rice is cooked and milk is almost mixed up with rice remove from flame.
- Let it cool.
- Serve garnishing with cherries.

72. NYs Rice To Riches Chocolate Chip Flirt Rice Pudding Recipe

Serving: 4 | Prep: | Cook: 10mins | Ready in:

Ingredients

- 1 liter full-cream milk
- 250 ml cream
- 1/2 orange, zest of
- 3/4 cup brown sugar
- 1/2 cup italian risotto rice

- 200 g coarsely chopped dark chocolate

Direction

- Put everything, except the chocolate, into a heavy based saucepan and bring to boil, stirring frequently.
- Simmer 30 minutes until rice is tender and mixture thick and creamy.
- Remove from heat and add chocolate. Stir a couple of times to give a ripple effect.
- Serve warm or cold.

73. No Bake Rice Pudding Recipe

Serving: 4 | Prep: | Cook: 60mins | Ready in:

Ingredients

- -4 cups milk
- -2 cups cooked rice
- -4 eggs
- -1/2 cup sugar
- -1 tsp. vanilla extract

Direction

- -in medium saucepan, heat milk and rice, stirring frequently so milk does not burn. Bring to a slow simmer.
- -in a separate bowl, combine eggs, sugar and vanilla. When rice has soaked up half of the milk, add egg mixture to the pot.
- -allow to cook for just a few more minutes or when there is only a little milk left, stirring occasionally.
- -eat while still hot or chill in the fridge and eat cold. Good for dessert or as a snack. Can also be made into a breakfast pudding by adding raisins, dates etc.

74. Orange Rice Pudding Recipe

Serving: 4 | Prep: | Cook: 5mins | Ready in:

Ingredients

- 2 c. white rice, cooked
- 1 1/2 c. heavy whipping cream
- 1 t. vanilla
- 1/2 the zest from 1 orange

Direction

- Cook rice according to package or use left over rice
- Over med. low heat add heavy whipping cream to rice. Bring to almost a boil, take off heat.
- Add vanilla and zest

75. PINA COLADA INSTANT RICE PUDDING Recipe

Serving: 8 | Prep: | Cook: 2mins | Ready in:

Ingredients

- 1 - 20 OUNCE CAN OF crushed pineapple
- I CUP instant rice
- 1 -3.4 - OUNCE- PACKAGE OF INSTANT banana CREAM PUDDING, OR vanilla
- 2 CUPS milk
- 1/2 CUP flaked coconut
- 1/2 CUP MINATURE MARSHMELLOWS
- 1/3 CUP CHOPPED nuts YOUR CHOICE
- 1 TABLESPOON lemon juice
- 1 banana SLICED

Direction

- DRAIN PINEAPPLE AND RESERVE THE JUICE.
- BRING JUICE AND 1/2 CUP OF WATER TO A BOIL, STIR IN RICE AND SIMMER 2 MINUTES,

- REMOVE FROM HEAT, COVER AND LET STEAM 5 MINUTES.
- PREPARE PUDDING, IN A MEDIUM BOWL, ACCORDING TO PACKAGE INSTRUCTIONS USING THE 2 CUPS OF MILK
- ADD PINEAPPLE, COCONUT, MARSHMELLOWS, NUTS AND LEMON JUICE, BANANA AND HOT RICE MIXTURE. STIR TO MIX
- CHILL 30 MINUTES OR MORE

76. Peachy Rice Pudding Recipe

Serving: 6 | Prep: | Cook: 30mins | Ready in:

Ingredients

- 1-1/3 cups water
- 2/3 cup long grain rice
- 3/4 cup evaporated milk
- 1/3 cup mixed dried fruit bits
- 2 teaspoons honey
- 1/4 teaspoon ground cinnamon
- 1/8 teaspoon salt
- 1 cup chopped peeled peaches
- 1/4 cup vanilla yogurt

Direction

- In medium saucepan stir together water and uncooked rice.
- Bring to boiling then reduce heat and simmer covered for 20 minutes.
- Stir evaporated milk, fruit bits, honey, cinnamon and salt into cooked rice.
- Bring just to boiling then reduce heat.
- Simmer uncovered over medium low heat 5 minutes stirring frequently.
- Serve pudding warm with peaches and yogurt.

77. Persimmon Rice Pudding Recipe

Serving: 0 | Prep: | Cook: 2hours | Ready in:

Ingredients

- 4 c. cooked rice, cooled**
- 2 c. American persimmon pulp
- 1 1/2 c. sugar
- 1 1/4 c. milk
- 1/3 c. all-purpose flour
- 1 egg, beaten
- 1 tsp. vanilla
- 1 1/2 tsp. cinnamon, optional
- 1/3 c. raisins
- 3/4 c. chopped nuts
- ** If you want to make this with brown rice, you'll need to find short-grain brown rice or sweet brown rice. Don't use long grain brown rice.

Direction

- Preheat oven to 350F. Butter a 3 quart casserole or a 9"x13" pan.
- Combine rice and persimmon pulp. Set aside.
- In a large mixing bowl combine sugar, milk, flour, egg, vanilla and optional cinnamon. Stir well to combine. Add rice and persimmon mixture. Mix well. Stir in nuts and raisins.
- Put in prepared casserole or pan, place in preheated oven and bake for 45 minutes, or until set.
- Serve warm with vanilla ice cream or cool with whipped topping or whipped cream.

78. Quickie Rice Pudding Recipe

Serving: 0 | Prep: | Cook: 30mins | Ready in:

Ingredients

- 1 Tbsp margarine or butter
- 1 cup uncooked extra long grain white rice

- 2 cups water
- 1 1/2 cups raisins
- 1 (4-serving) box regular or sugar free instant vanilla pudding
- 2 cups milk
- 1/4 tsp ground nutmeg, plus extra for garnishing

Direction

- 1. Melt butter in a 2 qt. saucepan. Pour in rice and let it brown just lightly before pouring in water. Add raisins and bring to a boil.
- 2. Turn the heat down to medium low and cover with a vented lid. Set timer for 14 minutes. It will be done when there's "holes" in the rice mixture. Put in the refrigerator to cool, or do it quickly by setting the pan in a bowl full of ice cubes.
- 3. Meanwhile, make the pudding with the milk, and add the 1/4 tsp. nutmeg. In a large serving bowl, add the cooled down rice mixture to the pudding and combine.
- 4. Serve room temp or chilled, with a sprinkle of extra nutmeg, if desired.
- YIELD: 6 to 8 servings

79. Raisin Rice Pudding Recipe

Serving: 8 | Prep: | Cook: 90mins | Ready in:

Ingredients

- 6 Tablespoons sugar, divided
- 2 envelopes unflavored gelatin
- 1/2 teaspoon nutmeg
- 1/2 teaspoon salt
- 2 1/2 cups milk, divided
- 1/4 cup long grain rice
- 1/2 cup raisins (I like the golden raisins)
- 3 eggs separated
- 1 cup heavy cream
- ~~RASPBERRY SAUCE~~
- 1 package (10 ounces) frozen raspberries (thawed)
- 1/4 cup ruby port
- 1 Tablespoon cornstarch
- 1/8 teaspoon salt
- 1/8 teaspoon almond extract

Direction

- Mix 4 tablespoons sugar with gelatine, nutmeg and salt in a large saucepan.
- Slowly stir in 2 cups milk until smooth.
- Add rice and raisins and bring to a boil.
- Reduce heat, cover, and simmer for 20 minutes, until rice is tender, stirring occasionally.
- Beat egg yolks and remaining 1/2 cup milk together
- Slowly add some of the hot rice mixture to egg yolk mixture, beating constantly
- Pour this back into the saucepan and mix all well.
- Refrigerate until cool and will mound when dropped from a spoon.
- About 1 1/2 hours.
- THEN:
- Beat the egg whites until foamy, add remaining 2 Tablespoons sugar and beat until stiff peaks form
- Fold into cooled rice mixture
- Beat the heavy cream until soft peaks form then fold into rice mixture
- Spoon pudding into 6 cup mold or bowl
- Refrigerate for 6 hours, or until firmly set
- Loosen pudding around edge and invert onto dessert platter
- Serve with Raspberry Sauce
- ~RASPBERRY SAUCE
- Thaw the raspberries and strain juice into small saucepan, reserving raspberries.
- Stir in port, cornstarch, and salt until smooth.
- Heat to boiling stirring constantly, boil one minute
- Cool to room temperature
- Stir in almond extract then fold in reserved raspberries

80. Rice And Lentil Pudding Recipe

Serving: 10 | Prep: | Cook: 15mins | Ready in:

Ingredients

- 1 C milk plus 3 1/2 C water
- 1 C raw rice
- 1/3 C split green bean (Mung Dal) , roasted in 1/2 tbsp butter (OPTIONAL)
- 1 C jaggery in 1/4 C water boiled until thread consistency .
- 1 tbsp nuts and raisins roasted in 1 tbsp butter
- 2 cardamom , crushed

Direction

- Boil the milk mixed with water.
- Add the rice and dhal to it.
- Simmer for 10 mins.
- Add the nuts, raisins and cardamoms.
- Once fully cooked and sticky, mix the syrup in.
- Serve piping HOT.

81. Rice Custard Pudding Recipe

Serving: 8 | Prep: | Cook: 85mins | Ready in:

Ingredients

- 1/2 cup long grain white rice
- 1-1/2 cups water
- 1/2 tsp salt
- 1/3 cup sugar
- 3 eggs
- 2 tsp vanilla
- 1/2 cup or more raisins
- 3/4 tsp grated lemon rind
- 3-1/2 cup milk
- 1 tsp nutmeg
- 2-3 tbsp cinnamon
- 2 tbsp butter

Direction

- Preheat oven to 300
- Cook rice in salted water till tender, then drain.
- In a medium bowl beat eggs slightly. Stir in sugar, vanilla, raisins, lemon rind, nutmeg & cinnamon.
- In another bowl combine milk & cooked rice.
- Add rice mixture to egg mixture.
- Pour into a 2 quart casserole pan. Sprinkle with more nutmeg and cinnamon to your taste. Then dot with butter. (I add one cinnamon stick in the middle)
- Set casserole in a baking pan; fill baking pan with about 1" hot water
- Bake uncovered about 1 hour and 25 minutes, stirring once after the first half hour.
- To avoid breaking the top of crust, insert spoon at edge of pudding, draw gently back and forth along bottom of the casserole. Near the end of baking time, insert a silver knife in center of custard, if it comes out clean, custard is done.
- Remove casserole from baking pan and cool.

82. Rice Festival Pudding Recipe

Serving: 2 | Prep: | Cook: 10mins | Ready in:

Ingredients

- 1/2 cup long grain rice
- 1 cup water
- 1/2 teaspoon salt
- 1 quart milk
- 1/2 stick butter
- 3 eggs beaten
- 1/2 cup granulated sugar
- 1 cup seedless raisins
- 1/2 teaspoon vanilla extract

Direction

- Add rice and salt to boiling water in a large sauce pan.
- Cover and cook over low heat for 10 minutes.

- Add milk and butter and bring to boil.
- Turn heat to very low and when milk has ceased boiling cover and cook for 1 hour.
- Add sugar, raisins and vanilla to beaten eggs then pour into the rice stirring slowly for 3 minutes.

83. Rice Pudding Euphoria Recipe

Serving: 6 | Prep: | Cook: 30mins | Ready in:

Ingredients

- • 1 cup cooked brown or white rice
- • 1 cup brown sugar
- • 1 14 oz. can coconut cream or milk (unsweetened)
- • 1/8 cup cassava (or tapioca) flour
- • 1/8 teaspoon salt
- • 1 teaspoon ground cinnamon
- • 1/4 cup of minced candied ginger, raisins or any other fruit you might like (optional)
- • 1/4 cup chopped nuts (optional)
- • 1 teaspoon vanilla

Direction

- Mix everything but the vanilla together in a saucepan and bring to a boil over medium heat, stirring occasionally.
- Reduce heat to low.
- Cook, stirring occasionally, until thick (about 1 hour).
- Mix in vanilla and serve warm, or put into individual bowls and chill for at least an hour before serving.

84. Rice Pudding KHEER Recipe

Serving: 8 | Prep: | Cook: 25mins | Ready in:

Ingredients

- 1 cup water
- 1/2 cup basmati rice
- 4 cups whole milk
- 1 tsp. raisins (optional)
- 2 tsp. cashews and pistachios (optional)
- 10 to 12 treads of saffron (you may soak them in one teaspoon of milk for two hours) (optional)
- 3 small pieces green cardamom, crushed with one teaspoon of sugar (If you crush cardamom with sugar, then it is easier to grind and increases flavor and aroma) 1/4cup of sugar (or to taste)

Direction

- Soak rice in water for 2 hours.
- Boil milk.
- Add rice to it.
- Boil slowly for 30 minutes or more until the mixture reaches a slightly thick consistency, but you can stir it easily.
- Add sugar and mix it well. Cook for 5 minutes more. It will thicken a little more.
- Put off pan from fire and let it cool. Cooling will increase its thick consistency more.
- Add saffron (which had been soaked in milk), raisins, cashews and pistachios.

85. Rice Pudding Recipe

Serving: 12 | Prep: | Cook: 150mins | Ready in:

Ingredients

- 1 quart whole milk
- 1/4 cup rice (sometimes I up it to 1/3 cup!)
- 1/2 cup sugar
- 1/2 teaspoon salt
- 1/2 cup raisins
- 1 teaspoon vanilla
- 1/4 teaspoon nutmeg

Direction

- Preheat oven to 350 degrees F.
- Combine milk, rice, sugar and salt in a 6-cup, well-buttered casserole dish.
- Bake, uncovered, for 2 hours.
- Stir pudding every 1/2 hour.
- Remove from oven after 2 hours.
- Stir in raisins, vanilla and nutmeg.
- Mix well.
- Bake 1/2 hour longer without stirring.
- Serve sprinkled with nutmeg or cinnamon and a dollop of whipped cream.

86. Rice Pudding Upgraded Recipe

Serving: 8 | Prep: | Cook: 20mins | Ready in:

Ingredients

- 2/3 cup water
- 2/3 cup Minute Rice
- dash of salt
- 1 1/2 cup whole milk
- 1 egg yolk slightly beaten
- 1/3 cup sugar
- 1/3 cup raisins
- 1/8 tsp cinnamon
- 1/8 tsp nutmeg
- 1 tbsp butter

Direction

- Add the salt to the water and bring to a rolling boil
- Stir in the rice, cover and remove from heat
- Let stand 5 minutes
- Blend the egg yolk and milk
- Mix egg and milk thoroughly into the rice
- Add sugar and raisins
- Add the cinnamon, nutmeg and butter
- Mix well
- Return to heat
- Heat until boiling again, stirring constantly
- Remove from heat
- Let stand at least 1 hour

- This dish may be served cold or warm.

87. Rice Pudding With Cherries And Almonds Recipe

Serving: 6 | Prep: | Cook: 280mins | Ready in:

Ingredients

- 3/4 cup/175 mL granulated sugar
- 1/2 cup/125 mL arborio rice (see Tips, below)
- 1/4 cup/50 mL dried cherries (see Tips, below)
- 2 tbsp/25 mL ground almonds
- 1 tsp/5 mL grated lemon zest
- Pinch salt
- 4 cups/1 L milk (see Tips, below)
- 2 eggs
- 1 tsp/5 mL almond extract
- toasted sliced almonds, optional
- whipped cream, optional

Direction

- In greased slow cooker stoneware, mix together sugar, rice, cherries, almonds, lemon zest and salt.
- In a large bowl, whisk together milk, eggs and almond extract, and stir into rice mixture. Cover and cook on High for 4 hours, until rice is tender and pudding is set. Serve warm or cover and chill. Garnish with toasted almonds and whipped cream, if desired.
- TIPS
- Long-grain white rice can be successfully used in this recipe, but the pudding will not be as creamy as one made with Arborio rice.
- Use 1 cup (250 mL) fresh pitted cherries in place of the dried cherries, if desired. Or substitute an equal quantity of dried cranberries instead.
- For a richer pudding, use half milk and half cream.

88. Rice Pudding My Way Recipe

Serving: 0 | Prep: | Cook: 22mins | Ready in:

Ingredients

- 1 litre (4 cups) whole milk, plus more as required
- 100 g (3.5 oz) short grained rice (soaked for half an hour)
- sugar-as much/little as you want
- 1 can (400 g/14 oz) sweetened condensed milk
- 1tsp cardamom powder
- ½ cup mixed dried fruit and nuts (like raisins, almonds, cashews)
- a few strands of saffron dissolved in 1 tbsp of warm milk
- 1 tbsp clarified butter

Direction

- Boil the milk, condensed milk and sugar in a deep, heavy-bottomed dish.
- When the milk comes to a boil, add the rice and simmer. Cook till the milk thickens and reduces to half its original volume.
- Heat the butter in a wok and roast your dry fruits. Add them (reserve some for garnishing) to your pudding mix and cook for another 5 mins.
- Take it off the heat and add the saffron. Stir well.
- Allow it to cool.
- Garnish with the remaining dry fruits.
- Chill before serving.

89. Ris À La Malta (Jonsson All Time Favorite) Recipe

Serving: 0 | Prep: | Cook: 30mins | Ready in:

Ingredients

- 1 Tbsp. butter
- pinch of salt
- 1 cup short-grained, glutinous rice (I like to use Jasmine because of its added sweetness; pearl rice also works well)
- 2 cups full cream milk. (I use 1:2 ratio, 1c rice to 2 c milk)
- 1 1/2 cups heavy cream (I use one tetra brick of all purpose cream)
- 1 tsp. ground cinnamon or 1 cinnamon stck
- 1 tbsp sugar to taste (optional)

Direction

- 1. Melt butter in small pot in low fire.
- 2. Put glutinous rice. Stir occasionally to coat rice with butter and avoid rice from sticking in bottom of pot.
- 3. Pour 1/2 cup milk, pinch of salt and sprinkle cinnamon powder. You can add sugar if you prefer sweeter porridge. (Cinnamon gives your porridge a nice aroma and brownish color)
- 4. Let it simmer over low fire, stirring occasionally to avoid porridge from becoming lumpy.
- 5. When rice is half cooked, pour in remaining milk and continue stirring. Let simmer for another 5 minutes
- 6. Then pour in cream, stir and simmer until rice is cooked. (You may notice some sticky rice forming in bottom of your pot. No worries it happens. DO not stir too much so the sticky rice in bottom will not mix with your porridge.)
- 7. Serve warm or cold. Best with sliced fruits, berries or bacon bits.
- ** You can add more milk if you prefer thinner consistency.
- *** You can skip the sugar if you prefer a less sweet porridge

90. Risotto Rice Pudding Recipe

Serving: 6 | Prep: | Cook: 180mins | Ready in:

Ingredients

- 1/2 cup arborio rice
- 8 cups whole milk
- 1/2 cup sugar
- 1 vanilla bean, split in half lengthwise
- 1/4 teaspoon cinnamon
- 1/4 teaspoon salt
- 2 large egg yolks
- 1/2 cup heavy cream
- 2 teaspoons vanilla extract
- Freshly grated nutmeg (optional)

Direction

- Combine rice, milk, sugar, vanilla bean, cinnamon and salt in a large, heavy-bottomed saucepan over medium high heat.
- Bring mixture to a boil, stirring constantly.
- Reduce heat to medium low and simmer, stirring every 5 minutes as the mixture starts to thicken.
- Continue this for about 30 minutes.
- Continue cooking until the rice is tender but not mushy, about 15 minutes longer.
- The milk will be thick and the rice tender; the mixture will a little soupy.
- As pudding cools it thickens.
- If too thick while still hot, it will cool to a stodgy lump with no creaminess.
- Whisk egg yolks and cream together in a bowl.
- Stir slowly into pudding.
- Continue cooking pudding over medium low heat for 2 to 3 minutes until eggs are cooked through and pudding is creamy, glossy and still fairly soupy.
- Remove from heat and stir in vanilla.
- Grate a little nutmeg into pudding, if desired.
- Remove vanilla bean.
- Pour pudding into serving bowl and press plastic wrap over the surface to prevent a skin from forming.
- Refrigerate until cold, at least 2 to 3 hours.

- Serve cold.
- NOTE: This pudding is delicious as is or you can fold a dollop of whipped cream into each serving.

91. Rocky Road Rice Pudding Recipe

Serving: 4 | Prep: | Cook: 10mins | Ready in:

Ingredients

- 2-1/2 cups milk
- 1/2 cup instant rice
- 1 package regular vanilla pudding mix
- 1/2 cup tiny marshmallows
- 1/2 cup semisweet chocolate pieces
- 1/4 cup chopped walnuts

Direction

- In medium saucepan combine milk and rice then bring just to boiling over medium heat.
- Stir in pudding mix then cook stirring constantly until mixture comes to a full boil.
- Remove from heat then cover and let stand 5 minutes.
- Stir in marshmallows, chocolate and walnuts then pour into six dessert dishes.
- Cool at room temperature for 1 hour before serving garnished with additional marshmallows.

92. Rose Rice Pudding Recipe

Serving: 4 | Prep: | Cook: 20mins | Ready in:

Ingredients

- 4 tbsp basmati rice
- 3/4 cup sugar (adjust to taste)
- 3 cups milk
- 2 tbsp rose water

- 1 tbsp rose petal jam/gulkand
- 4 cardamoms, powdered
- crushed almonds and pistachios for garnish

Direction

- Wash and soak rice in water for 30 minutes.
- Grind the rice to a paste with a little water.
- Boil milk in a pan with cardamom powder.
- When it starts boiling add rice paste and stir to avoid lumps.
- Stir in the sugar. Cook for ten to fifteen minutes until the milk thickens considerably (this is usually thick and custard-like).
- Add rose water.
- Remove from heat and add rose petal jam after a few minutes.
- Pour into individual bowls, garnish with crushed nuts and serve chilled.

93. Roz Bel Laban Rice Pudding Recipe

Serving: 4 | Prep: | Cook: 25mins | Ready in:

Ingredients

- 1 cup white rice
- 2 cups water
- 3 cups whole milk, or reconstituted non-dairy creamer*
- 1 cup granulated sugar, or sugar substitute**
- 1 tablespoon orange blossom water
- powdered cinnamon
- * If you use powdered non-dairy creamer, reconstitute it by placing 2 to 3 tablespoons creamer in hot water, stir to dissolve, and let cool.
- ** If you use reconstituted creamer, reduce the sweetener amount to 3/4 cup.

Direction

- In a large saucepan, cook rice in water for 15 minutes.

- Add milk (or creamer), and stir until the mixture becomes thick.
- Add orange blossom water and sugar. Continue stirring until rice is done.
- Place in individual serving bowls and sprinkle with cinnamon, or place in large serving dish and sprinkle with cinnamon.
- Serve when cool or chill in refrigerator.

94. Rum Raisin Rice Pudding Recipe

Serving: 4 | Prep: | Cook: 30mins | Ready in:

Ingredients

- 1 cup arborio rice
- 3 cups milk
- 4 sticks cinnamon
- 1 can condensed milk
- 1 vanilla bean
- 3/4 cup dark rum
- 1/4 cup water
- 1 cup jumbo golden raisins

Direction

- In a heavy medium sauce pan bring milk and cinnamon sticks to a boil over medium heat. Add rice, return to a boil then simmer for 15 minutes, stirring occasionally.
- While rice is cooking place the rum, 1/4 cup water and raisins in a small pot. Bring to a boil, then turn the heat to simmer and cook until almost all the liquid is absorbed, (you want some left over to mix into the rice when it's finished). Set aside to cool.
- Add condensed milk and scrape vanilla bean into the rice. Continue to cook over low heat stirring often for an additional 15 minutes or so or until rice is creamy, but still has some liquid left in the pot. It will still seem rather soupy, but in order for it to be very creamy when cool, you remove it from the heat at this stage.

- The rice pudding will keep for 1 week covered in the refrigerator.

95. Rum Raisin Slow Cooker Rice Pudding Recipe

Serving: 14 | Prep: | Cook: 6hours | Ready in:

Ingredients

- 7 cups milk
- 1 plus 1/4 cup half and half
- 1 cup long grain white rice or arborio rice
- 1 c sugar
- 3 eggs
- 2 tsp vanilla
- 1/2 tsp cinnamon - or you can add a little more
- 1/4 tsp salt
- 1 cup raisins, soaked in rum for several hours, or add more if u love them
- 1/4 tsp Grated orange or lemon peel (optional)

Direction

- Butter the inside of a 4 qt. or larger slow cooker
- Turn it on high and put 1 cup half and half plus 7 cups milk, sugar and rice in there and cook for 4 hours or until the rice is tender. I really think it depends on your cooker, mine runs hot and it was more like 3 hours. When the rice is tender, remove 1/2 cup of it into a bowl. In another large bowl, combine eggs, cinnamon, salt, vanilla and remaining 1/4 c half and half. (You can omit the half and half here if you want and just do an egg mixture if you like more rice texture to your pudding. You can even use 1 less egg for more rice texture) Mix the rice slowly into the egg mixture. Repeat this process, adding 1/2 c of the rice into the egg mixture until the crock pot is half empty, stirring well. Then add it all back into the crock pot and stir again. (Tempering your eggs is what this is called so

that they don't wind up as scrambled eggs when you add them) Lastly, add the rum soaked raisins and cook for about another 20 to 30 minutes on high. You can put the raisins in a pan and light the rum liquid to burn off some of the alcohol, and I kind of recommend doing that if you will be serving the pudding shortly after it's cooked. Definitely drain the raisins before adding them, but you can use rum instead of the vanilla too if you want to intensify the rum flavor. Other options include putting in the soaked raisins in during the last 45 min or hour of cooking the rice on high. Serve pudding warm or chilled. Don't be tempted to add more salt, but if you do keep it to 1/2 tsp. total. I've fooled around with salt with this recipe and you don't need much of it in there.

96. Rum Rasin Rice Pudding Recipe

Serving: 6 | Prep: | Cook: 45mins | Ready in:

Ingredients

- 2 1/2 cups rice
- 4 cups milk
- 2 cups half and half/heavy cream
- 1/2 cup sugar
- 1 can sweetened condensed milk
- 2 eggs
- 2 tbsp vanilla
- 3/4 cup rasins
- 1/2 cup rum
- nutmeg and cinnamon for garnish

Direction

- Combine rice, milk, half and half, and sugar in a wide bottomed pot, bring to a near boil and stir constantly
- Combine raisins and rum in a small pan, put on med heat until raisins are plumped and juicy, and remove from heat

- Beat the two eggs and set aside
- When the rice is 3/4 cooked, stir in the condensed milk
- When the rice is fully cooked, temper your eggs (add small liquid from the rice 2-3 ounces at a time while stirring to bring the eggs up to temperature) and then slowly pour into the rice mixture and stir until incorporated
- Add raisins and remaining rum to the rice mixture
- Cook for 5 minutes more to cook the eggs while stirring constantly
- Pour into a casserole dish
- Sprinkle some nutmeg and cinnamon overtop to garnish
- Let sit till it cools a bit, and serve while warm

97. Scrumptious Vegan Red Rice Pudding Recipe

Serving: 0 | Prep: | Cook: 1hours | Ready in:

Ingredients

- 3 -4 cups of overcooked red rice
- 2 cups water
- 1 cup raw cashews
- 4 tbsp maple syrup
- 1 tbsp vanilla essence
- 2 tsp stevia

Direction

- Put the rice on to cook (follow instructions on the pack)
- I always use the absorption method
- Blend all the other ingredients to make a sweet cashew milk
- When rice is overcooked, i.e. rice pudding consistency
- Pour in sweetened vanilla cashew milk
- It is good to add it while rice is still very warm
- Let sit for 10 minutes for flavours to mingle
- Serve

98. Simple Rice Pudding Recipe

Serving: 6 | Prep: | Cook: 20mins | Ready in:

Ingredients

- 2 cups cooked rice
- 2.5 cups of whole milk
- 1/3-1/2 cup of brown sugar(depends on taste)
- 2 green cardamom pods crushed
- 1/2 tsp clove
- 1.5 tsp cinnamon
- 1 tsp freshly grated ginger
- a pinch of salt

Direction

- Combine all ingredients and bring to a boil. Simmer until nice and thick making sure to constantly stir. (Takes about 20 minutes)

99. Slow Cooked Kheer Rice Pudding Recipe

Serving: 8 | Prep: | Cook: 360mins | Ready in:

Ingredients

- 1 Cup rice (I use basmati)
- 2-1/2 Cups water
- A pinch of salt
- 1/2 Gallon milk (about 2 litres)
- 2 to 2-1/2 Cups sugar
- 1/2 Cup raisins
- 10 - 12 pieces pistachios (powdered)
- 1/4 Cup slivered almonds
- A few drops kewra (screwpine) essence or rose water

Direction

- Wash rice, soak and keep aside.

- In a medium saucepan bring water to a boil, add salt. Drain soaked rice and add to boiling water. Cook until well done about 15 minutes.
- Add cooked rice into a 4 qt. crock pot (slow cooker), add milk. Make sure that the milk remains at least 2 inches below the rim of the cooker. Stir once and set to cook on High for about 5-1/2 hours.
- Stir occasionally. After 5-1/2 hours when the rice and milk have come together add almonds, raisins and sugar. Stir thoroughly and cook on high again for at least 30 minutes.
- Turn off the heat and add kewra or rose water. Transfer the kheer into a serving dish and garnish with almonds and powdered pistachios (you can use whole or flaked ones too). Serve chilled.

100. South Indian Milk Rice Pudding Recipe

Serving: 5 | Prep: | Cook: 20mins | Ready in:

Ingredients

- Milk- 6 cups
- Basmati Indian Rice - 1/2 cup
- condensed milk - half tin
- Sugar - half cup
- cashew nuts - 1/2 cup (sliced lengthwise)
- Raisins - 1/4 cup (chopped)
- almonds - 1/4 cup (chopped)
- cardamom powder - 1/2 tsp
- cinnamon powder - 1/2 tsp

Direction

- Mix together 2 cups of water and 2 cups of milk and boil.
- Add rice to it and cook well.
- Add the remaining milk, condensed milk and sugar and allow it to boil.
- When it begins to thicken, add the other ingredients and stir continuously till it thickens again.

- Before serving, sprinkle the cardamom and cinnamon powders.

101. Southern Rice Pudding Recipe

Serving: 8 | Prep: | Cook: 50mins | Ready in:

Ingredients

- 1 cup uncooked rice
- 4 cups milk
- 2 tablespoons butter
- 1 cup granulated sugar
- 4 eggs
- 1/4 teaspoon cinnamon
- 1/4 teaspoon mace
- 1 lemon rind grated

Direction

- Soak rice in 2 cups milk for 2 hours then add remaining milk and cook over low 20 minutes.
- Set aside to cool then heat oven to 350 and butter a 2 quart casserole.
- Work butter until soft then work in sugar thoroughly and beat eggs until frothy.
- Add sugar mixture and rice then flavor with cinnamon, mace and lemon rind.
- Pour into casserole and bake for 45 minutes then serve warm.

102. Spicy Orange Rice Pudding Recipe

Serving: 12 | Prep: | Cook: 50mins | Ready in:

Ingredients

- 10 cups whole milk
- 250 g. long or short grain white rice
- 1/2 teaspoon salt

- 1 cup granulated sugar
- 1 teaspoon pure vanilla extract
- 2 teaspoon orange blossom water
- 1 teaspoon ground cinnamon
- 1 teaspoon ground ginger
- 1/2 teaspoon allspice
- 1 cup brown or golden raisins, or/and chopped pistachios(optional)
- Lightly sweetened whipped cream
- Orange citrus curls to decorate

Direction

- In a medium heavy bottomed saucepan combine the milk, rice, cinnamon sticks and salt. Place saucepan over high heat and bring to a boil. Reduce the heat to medium to medium-low and simmer until the rice is tender (about 25 minutes).
- Stir the milk mixture frequently using a heatproof rubber spatula or wooden spoon to prevent the rice from sticking to the bottom of the pan. When the rice is tender, remove from heat and add the sugar, vanilla extract, ginger, allspice, orange blossom water, and ground cinnamon. Return to heat and cook until the rice pudding thickens, about 5 to 10 minutes. Remove from heat and add the raisins or/and pistachios (optional)
- Spoon the pudding into your serving bowls and cover with plastic wrap. If you want a film or skin on the puddings, allow them to cool before covering with plastic wrap. Refrigerate until serving time, about to 2 hours.
- If desired, garnish with lightly sweetened whipped cream.
- Decorate with orange citrus curls

---

103.   Stove Top Rice Pudding Recipe

Serving: 0 | Prep: | Cook: 40mins | Ready in:

Ingredients

- 1/2 cup white rice, short or medium grain
- 1 Qt half & half
- 3/4 cup sugar
- 1 Tbsp cornstarch
- 1/4 tsp salt
- 4 eggs
- 1 tsp vanilla
- 1/2 cup raisins or dried sour cherries (optional)
- 1/4 tsp cinnimon (optional)

Direction

- Cook rice according to directions, until tender.
- While rice is cooking, combine sugar, salt, cornstarch, vanilla and eggs in a mixing bowl and beat together by hand.
- In a 3 qt. sauce pan put sugar & egg mixture together with half & half and heat on medium - low, stirring constantly. (Takes about 20 - 25 minutes)
- When rice is cooked add it to the pudding mixture. (This is where you add the raisins or cherries)
- When pudding is consistency of a very thick gravy, it is done. Pour into a bowl or smaller serving bowls. Sprinkle with cinnamon, cool and serve.

---

104.   Stovetop Rice Pudding Recipe

Serving: 4 | Prep: | Cook: 35mins | Ready in:

Ingredients

- 2 Tbsp butter
- 1/2 c short grain rice
- 1/4 tsp ground cardamom
- 1/4 tsp cinnamon
- 21/2 c milk (i use skim) but use what you like
- 2 Tbsp sugar
- 1 tsp finely grated orange peel
- A handful of raisins!! i almost forgot!!!

Direction

- In small saucepan, melt butter over medium heat. Add rice, cardamom and cinnamon; stir to coat.
- Stir in milk raisins and sugar; bring to boil. Reduce heat, cover and simmer, stirring often, until most of the liquid is absorbed and rice is tender, about 25 minutes.
- Stir in orange rind. Serve warm.

105. Thai Sticky Mango Rice Recipe

Serving: 4 | Prep: | Cook: 25mins | Ready in:

Ingredients

- 115 g sticky (glutinous) white rice
- 3/4 cup thick coconut milk
- 3 tbsp granulated sugar
- pinch of salt
- 2 ripe mangoes
- strips of lime rind, to decorate

Direction

- Rinse the glutinous rice thoroughly in several changes of cold water, then leave to soak overnight in a bowl of fresh, cold water.
- Drain and spread the rice in an even layer in a steamer lined with cheesecloth. Cover and steam for about 20 minutes or until the grains of rice are tender.
- Reserve 3 tbsp. of the top of the coconut milk and combine the rest with the sugar and salt in a saucepan. Bring to the boil, stirring until the sugar dissolves, then pour into a bowl and leave to cool a little.
- Turn the rice into a bowl and pour over the coconut mixture. Stir, then leave for about 10 - 15 minutes.
- Peel the mangoes and cut the flesh into slices. Place on top of the rice and drizzle over the reserved coconut milk. Decorate with strips of lime rind.

106. Tia Mildred's Arroz Con Leche (My Aunt Mildred's Rice Pudding) Recipe

Serving: 6 | Prep: | Cook: 35mins | Ready in:

Ingredients

- 3/4 C short Grain white rice
- 3 C water
- 1 Med cinnamon stick
- 2 1/4 C milk
- 1/4 tsp salt
- 2/3 C sugar
- ground cinnamon

Direction

- Bring the water and cinnamon stick to a boil in a heavy saucepan.
- Rinse the rice until water runs clear. Drain and stir into the saucepan. Reduce the heat to low and cook uncovered for 15 mins or until the rice absorbed the water.
- Mix the milk with the sugar and salt. Add to the rice and stir. Bring to a boil.
- Reduce the heat to moderate and cook uncovered for 15 mins or until it thickens. Stir occasionally.
- Served sprinkled with the ground cinnamon.

107. Turkish Rice Pudding Sutlac Recipe

Serving: 4 | Prep: | Cook: 24mins | Ready in:

Ingredients

- Sutlac (Turkish rice Pudding)

- 1/2 pound rice
- 4 cups milk
- 1 Cup sugar (if you dont like sweet use 1/2half)
- 1 teaspoon vanilla
- 1 teaspoon salt

Direction

- * Take a half-pound of short-grain or "pudding" rice and soak it for 30 minutes. Drain and rinse it. Put the rice in a pan, cover it with water, and cook, uncovered, until almost all the water has been absorbed.
- * Stir in 4 cups milk and simmer gently until the mixture thickens.
- * Add 1 lb. of sugar, and salt cook it gently for 23 to minutes, stirring occasionally.
- * It should be thicker than a pouring consistency, but not solid.
- * Stir in 1 teaspoon vanilla extract pour the mixture into a small bowl sprinkle on the cinnamon Serve at cold

108. White Chocolate Rice Pudding With Dried Cranberry Compote Recipe

Serving: 6 | Prep: | Cook: 12mins | Ready in:

Ingredients

- white chocolate rice pudding with dried cranberry compote
- I am sure you can do without the cranberries if you like.
- Servings: Serves 6.
- Ingredients
- 4 1/2 cups whole milk
- 2/3 cup long-grain white rice
- 2/3 cup sugar
- 1 tablespoon vanilla extract
- 1/4 teaspoon salt
- 2 large egg yolks

- 3 tablespoons whipping cream
- 4 ounces good-quality white chocolate (such as Lindt or Baker's), chopped
- 1 tablespoon grated orange peel
- 3/4 teaspoon ground cardamom
- Dried Cranberry Compote

Direction

- Preparation
- Combine first 5 ingredients in heavy large saucepan. Cook over medium-low heat until mixture thickens and rice is very tender, stirring occasionally, about 1 hour.
- Reduce heat to low. Whisk egg yolks and cream in small bowl. Gradually whisk in 1/2 cup rice mixture; return to same pan and cook 2 minutes, stirring constantly (do not boil). Remove from heat. Add chocolate; stir until melted. Stir in orange peel and cardamom. Transfer pudding to bowl; cover and chill until cold. (Can be prepared 1 day ahead. Keep refrigerated.)
- Spoon pudding into bowls. Top with Dried Cranberry Compote

109. White Sugar Rice Pudding Cake Recipe

Serving: 6 | Prep: | Cook: 20mins | Ready in:

Ingredients

- 100 g rice flour, sifted
- 80 g white sugar
- 200 ml water
- ½ tsp active dry yeast
- ½ tbsp lukewarm water
- ¼ tsp baking powder

Direction

- Mix rice flour, water and sugar together in a mixing bowl.

- In a non-stick pan, cook over low heat until the mixture has thickened.
- Keep stirring to avoid any lump during cooking.
- Strain mixture and cool.
- Mix the yeast and warm water and add in the cooled rice mixture together with the baking powder.
- Rest for 6 or 8 hours at the room temperature.
- Grease a 6 inch steamer with vegetable oil and line with foil and pour in the rice mixture.
- Steam over the high heat with boiled water for about 20 minutes.
- Cool, remove and cut into wedges.

110. Whitehouse Rice Pudding Recipe

Serving: 0 | Prep: | Cook: 10mins | Ready in:

Ingredients

- 2 quarts milk
- 1 can evaporated milk
- 1 cupful of sugar
- 1 tablespoon butter
- 1 teaspoon of cinnamon
- pinch of nutmeg
- pinch of salt
- 1 cup of small to medium grain rice

Direction

- 1. Preheat oven to 350 degrees F.
- 2. In a deep pudding dish place all the above ingredients.
- 3. Put in oven and occasionally stir.
- 4. Should have a cream like consistency.
- 5. You can eat hot or cold.

111. Wild Rice Pudding Recipe

Serving: 6 | Prep: | Cook: 25mins | Ready in:

Ingredients

- 2 cups half & half
- 4 eggs
- 1/4 cup sugar
- 1 teaspoon ground cinnamon
- 1/8 teaspoon salt
- 1 teaspoon vanilla extract
- 1 1/2 cups well-cooked wild rice
- 1/2 cup golden raisins
- 1/2 cup chopped almonds

Direction

- Prep time does not include cooking of the wild rice.
- Preheat oven to 325 F.
- In a small saucepan, scald half & half; set aside.
- Beat eggs and sugar until frothy.
- Stir in cinnamon, salt, vanilla, wild rice, raisins and almonds.
- Gradually stir in half & half.
- Divide mixture evenly between six 6-ounce custard cups.
- Place in large metal baking pan; fill with hot water to within 1-inch of top of custard cups.
- Bake 25-30 minutes or until knife inserted near center comes out clean.
- Remove custard cups from pan.
- Serve warm or cold with whipped cream.

Index

Conclusion

Thank you again for downloading this book!

I hope you enjoyed reading about my book!

If you enjoyed this book, please take the time to share your thoughts and post a review on Amazon. It'd be greatly appreciated!

Write me an honest review about the book – I truly value your opinion and thoughts and I will incorporate them into my next book, which is already underway.

Thank you!

If you have any questions, **feel free to contact at:** _author@bisquerecipes.com_

Jane Wilson

bisquerecipes.com

Printed in Great Britain
by Amazon